£15.00 C13 W11

Healing Energy
Prayer & Relaxation

Books by Israel Regardie from New Falcon Publications

Complete Golden Dawn System of Magic
Hyatt Memorial Edition
by Dr. Israel Regardie, Christopher S. Hyatt, and Lon Milo DuQuette

This is the master compilation of the teachings of the Hermetic Order of the Golden Dawn, a much improved edition of the ground breaking four-volume set by Dr. Regardie that revolutionized the occult world in the late 1930s. This new edition includes a complete Index and detailed Table of Contents compiled by James Strain to assist readers in their studies. Includes the Order's instructions in Magic, Tarot, Qabalah, Astrology, Invocation, Enochian Magic, and Esoteric Doctrine, along with the Order's Initiation Rituals. This massive hard cover volume includes copious illustrations with several in full color.

ISBN-13: 978-1561841714 • 8.5 x 11 • Hardcover • 1272 pages • $300.00
Special Limited Leatherbound Edition • Signed by Lon DuQuette • $666.00

What You Should Know About the Golden Dawn
by Dr. Israel Regardie

Regardie's personal account of his experience with those secret societies which have exerted such a great influence on the development of modern Occultism, including The Hermetic Order of the Golden Dawn, The Rosicrucian Fraternity and The Masonic Lodge. From his close personal associations Regardie reveals the true nature and actions of such leading Occult authorities as Aleister Crowley, Dion Fortune, S.L. MacGregor Mathers, Dr. W.W. Wescott, and others. This sixth revised edition includes new material by several modern adepts of the Golden Dawn, documents from the period of Regardie's association with Aleister Crowley which demonstrate Regardie's involvement in both the OTO and the A∴A∴, and hitherto unpublished material from the Regardie archives.

ISBN-13: 978-1561840649 • 5.5 x 8.5 • Paperback • 288 pages • $16.95

AUDIO CDS by Israel Regardie

The Golden Dawn Audio CDs: Volume 1 $22.00
The Golden Dawn Audio CDs: Volume 2 $22.00
The Golden Dawn Audio CDs: Volume 3 $22.00
The Magic of Israel Regardie $22.00
The World of Enochian Magick: The Angelic Revelations $22.00

Available from New Falcon Publications
http://www.newfalcon.com

HEALING ENERGY PRAYER & RELAXATION

by
DR. ISRAEL REGARDIE

Introduction by
COLIN WILSON

With Contributions by
CHRISTOPHER S. HYATT, PH.D.
JAMES WASSERMAN
LON MILO DUQUETTE
AIMA

NEW FALCON PUBLICATIONS
Reno, NV

Published in 2009 by:
NEW FALCON PUBLICATIONS
316 California Avenue • Suite 543
Reno, NV 89509
www.newfalcon.com
email: info@newfalcon.com

Copyright © 1982, 1989, 2009 by New Falcon Publications
The Sacred Ritual of the Pentagram Copyright © 1979 by Foibles Press

All rights reserved. No part of this book,
in part or in whole, may be reproduced, transmitted,
or utilized, in any form or by any means, electronic or mechanical,
including photocopying, recording, or by any information storage
and retrieval system, without permission in writing
from the publisher, except for brief quotations
in critical articles, books and reviews.

ISBN 13: 978-1-56184-183-7
ISBN 10: 1-56184-183-8

Library of Congress Catalog Card Number: 82-83292

First Edition 1982
Second Revised Edition 1989
Third Revised Edition 2009

Cover art: *Alchemist at Prayer* by Heinrich Khunrath, 1604
Book design and production by Studio 31
www.studio31.com

Printed in the USA

Contents

Introduction by Colin Wilson	7
Preface by Israel Regardie	15
A Scientific Approach to Metaphysics	19
Perfect Relaxation	29
God's Presence and Relaxation	43
Prayer	52
Ecstacy	65
The Process of Fulfillment	78
Triumphant Prayers of the Ancients	89

Essays by Contributors

The Philosophy and Technique of Active Prayer and Surrender by Christopher S. Hyatt, Ph.D.	101
An Alternate Method of Prayer: The Middle Pillar as a Group Working by James Wasserman	107
The Sacred Ritual of the Pentagram by AIMA	118
A Pentagram Exercise by Lon Milo DuQuette	148

Memorial Notice

Since this book was last published in 1989, Christopher S. Hyatt, Ph.D. passed on in February, 2008.

His great friend and mentor, Dr. Israel Regardie celebrated his own Greater Feast in 1985, three years after Colin Wilson wrote the following introduction to this book .

Dr. Regardie and Dr. Hyatt were giants in their field, enriching the modern occult tradition with their wisdom and unique perspectives. Both were also energetic people whose enthusiasm for life was matched only by their sense of humor.

They are missed by family, friends and students, but the world has been brightened and enlightened by the spiritual contributions that will long outlast their physical bodies.

We wish them both well on their journey through Infinity.

Introduction

Colin Wilson

The author of this small and fascinating book is the last living representative of the great "occult tradition" of the late 19th century, whose major names include Madame Blavatsky, W.B. Yeats, MacGregor Mathers, A.E. Waite, Aleister Crowley and Dion Fortune. Even in such distinguished company, Regardie stands out as a figure of central importance.

Francis Israel Regardie was born in London on November 17, 1907, and moved with his family to America in 1921. He attended art school in Philadelphia until, in his own words, "I realized I was no artist." Fate had marked him out for a rather more strange and interesting career. He received its first intimations when he was fifteen years old, and saw a reference to Madame Blavatsky in a book belonging to his sister. Intrigued by the name, he looked it up, and learned about the eventful career of that tempestuous lady. "From then on," he says, "I was hooked." The interest in Madame Blavatsky extended to Hindu philosophy and to the practice of yoga, and by the time he was eighteen, Regardie was familiar with the major works on yoga.

So it was with considerable excitement that, at the house of an attorney friend in Washington D.C., he made the discovery of a new text on yoga by a man who unmistakably knew what he was talking about. The work—which was read aloud—was called, rather cryptically, *Part 1 of Book IV,* and was by one Aleister Crowley. Regardie was so excited that he wrote to Crowley at the address of the publisher. And he had totally forgotten about it when, some eight months later, he received a reply from Paris. Crowley suggested that Regardie should get in touch with his New York agent, a German named Karl Germer. Regardie went to New York to meet Germer, and found that this ex-Wehrmacht officer regarded Crowley with enormous admiration. He sold Regardie a set of a work called *The Equinox,* a magazine that Crowley had published between 1909 and 1914. And for the next few months, Regardie plunged into an altogether strange world of magic, mysticism, occult philosophy and Nietzschean aphorism, all tinged with a distinct flavor of the 1890s. The result was that two years later, in October 1928, Regardie sailed for France, and was met at the Gare St. Lazare by Crowley; "the Great Beast" had invited Regardie to become his secretary.

The next two or three years must have been a traumatic experience for the young Americanized Londoner. Crowley had just published his most important book, *Magick in Theory and Practice,* which had failed to attract much attention; a quarrel with the book's press-agent led to the agent telling the police that Crowley was a drug addict. As a result, Crowley was expelled from Paris, and his new secretary, who had failed to obtain a residence permit, was also ordered to leave.

Introduction

Because of his association with Crowley, he was not allowed to land in England—although he had a British passport—and had to go to Brussels. It took him six more months before he was allowed to land in England. There he moved in with Crowley and his wife at a house at Knockholt, in Kent, and began preparing some of Crowley's works for the press—Crowley had discovered a publisher called P.R. Stephensen, who ran Mandrake Press. Unfortunately, Crowley's reputation as the "wickedest man in the world" was now so firmly established that his books aroused widespread opposition among booksellers, and the press soon went bankrupt. Meanwhile, Regardie and Stephensen collaborated on a short book in defense of Crowley, *The Legend of Aleister Crowley*. It did nothing to improve Crowley's sinister reputation, or to improve the finances of Mandrake Press. And so Crowley went his own way, and Regardie went his.

He became the secretary to the writer Thomas Burke, author of the once-famous *Limehouse Nights,* and he also wrote his own first two books, *The Garden of the Pomegranates* and *The Tree of Life*. Both are studies in the Hebrew magical system, the Qabalah, and the latter is regarded by many as one of the most important books on "magic" ever written. It is dedicated "with poignant memory of what might have been, to Marsyas." The latter is Crowley. And it is sad to record that when Regardie sent copies of one of his books to Crowley, the latter received it with something less than appreciation, and made some unkind jokes, particularly about Regardie's adoption of the name Francis—a name that had been bestowed on him by a woman friend who, like Regardie, was an admirer of St. Francis. Regardie gave way to outraged vanity, and wrote Crowley a sarcastic letter, addressing him as "Alice," a possible reference to the "Beast's" homosexual inclinations as well as a diminutive of his name. The result was a complete break between the two; Crowley produced a scurrilous document about his ex-secretary, accusing him of theft and betrayal, which he circulated to all Regardie's friends and acquaintances. It says a great deal for Regardie's forgiving nature—and for his capacity for objective admiration—that he has reproduced this document in full in his later study of Crowley, *The Eye in the Triangle*.

After the publication of *The Tree of Life*, Regardie found himself at the center of a violent controversy. He had discussed some of the magical practices of the society known as the Golden Dawn, of which Crowley had been a highly disruptive member in the early years of the century. Some ex-members attacked him; others—like Dion Fortune—supported him. The upshot was that he was invited to join the Stella Matutina, a magical order based upon the original Golden Dawn. This he found an immense disappointment. As "magicians" the chiefs of the Stella Matutina struck him as ignorant and inept. In disgust, he left the order, and decided to publish the rituals of the Golden Dawn—an act that has earned him much odium in "occult" circles, although every student of the history of occultism remains in his debt.

These details are necessary so that readers of this book should understand something of Regardie's importance in the history of 20th century "occultism." The remainder may be told more briefly. Regardie remained in England until

Introduction

1937, continuing to study magic and alchemy, and writing another important text, *The Philosopher Stone*, about the mysteries of alchemy. This is one of the most interesting and exciting things he ever wrote; it is basically a Jungian interpretation of alchemy as a search for some kind of unity of being, an attempt to unite conscious and unconscious forces of the psyche. (It is all the more fascinating in that in more recent years, Regardie changed his mind to some extent, and came to believe that alchemy *is* an attempt at a chemical transformation of matter—I tell the whole story in my book *Mysteries*.) And, in 1937, recognizing that war was inevitable, Regardie returned to the United States. Here he threw himself into the study of psychology—he had undergone Freudian analysis in England—and became a lay analyst. When America entered the war, he enlisted in the army—a step he wryly admits to have been "a ghastly error." After the war, he obtained his doctorate in psychology, moved to California, and practiced Reichian therapy. He admits that this, "with Magick, has changed the course of my whole life." In 1980, he retired to Arizona, where he continues to write.

For many years now, I have been an avid reader of Regardie's books. The last one I read, *Foundations of Practical Magic*, was published in England in 1979. It fascinated me because it reveals that, with age, Regardie's mind becomes more clear and vigorous—a tribute to the disciplines to which he has devoted his life. But the chapter that impressed me most was not concerned with magic, but with meditation. It is a remarkable synthesis of all he knows about magic, meditation and psychotherapy.

Now for those who—understandably—regard magic as an absurd superstition, it is important to bear in mind Crowley's own definitions: "Magick is the Science and Art of causing Change to occur in conformity with the Will." He is echoing a remark of the great 19th century occultist Eliphas Levi, who wrote: "Would you learn to reign over yourself and others? Learn how to will." Many students of magic are, no doubt, attracted by its romantic aura, and enjoy indulging in a kind of wishful thinking. But I suspect that the true students of magic have all started from the same intuition: that in some absurd, paradoxical way, *human beings are far stronger than they realize*. Everyone knows that odd feeling we get at times that all is well, that nothing can go wrong. Just as there are days when nothing seems to go right, so there are days when we experience a feeling that is like the first smell of spring: an excitement that seems based on some knowledge, some recognition. The romantic poets of the 19th century were always experiencing these "moments of vision," and then wondering the next day whether it was all an illusion. "Magic" is first of all an attempt to achieve some kind of control over that inner world of intuition. It escapes us because we are so poor at focusing the attention. So one of the first steps in magical practice is to attempt to train the mind to *visualize*, to be capable of "conjuring up" (and it is interesting that we use this particular phrase about imagining) objects and scenes and giving them "the smell of reality." And this ability is, in fact, one of the basic psychological disciplines: that is to say that a person who had become accustomed to doing it at will would have achieved a far higher level of mental health

Introduction

than the rest of us. Students of ritual magic also believe that when a person has achieved this level of intensity, it is, to some extent, possible to "make things happen." The magician does not, like the wizard in "The Sorceror's Apprentice," turn brooms into water-carriers; but he believes that it is possible to shape his own destiny. Again, everyone knows the feeling of being completely determined to do something, and how, when this happens, events often seem to "come out right." Jung would probably say that this is the operation of the immense unknown forces of the unconscious mind.

Regardie believes, as I do, that this knowledge is very old indeed—that it was probably already old when the Egyptians built their first temples. One of the most exciting things in the world is to discover that the latest findings in psychology, in structural linguistics, in split-brain physiology, blend smoothly into the pattern of the earliest recorded human knowledge. It is this insight that pervades this book on healing energy, prayer and relaxation and which makes it, to me, the most personal and moving of all Regardie's writings.

England
May 1982

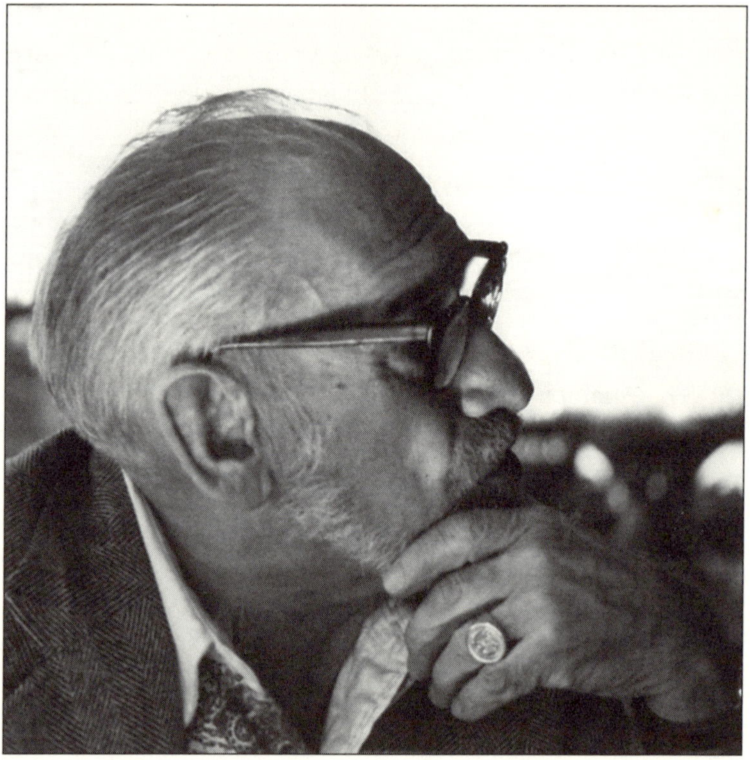

Preface

Israel Regardie

Countless books have already been written and published on prayer and relaxation. Why the need for another?

Many years devoted to varied forms of psychotherapy, as well as prolonged exposure to mysticism and allied topics, are the main factors that have led me to a rather different approach to this topic.

In the course of my professional life, what struck me vividly was that when people were enabled to shuffle off the unconscious armor of gross muscular tension, thus achieving a never-before-experienced delight and pleasure in the relaxation of psyche and soma, entirely new attitudes towards religion and prayer spontaneously developed. They needed no orientation, no preparation, no coaching. It was just there. And a whole new life of fervor, inspiration and prayer made its appearance. Not prayer in the conventional institutionalized form, but an intimacy with Life and Love that was intense, devout, springing from wells deep within the psyche.

It would seem that once the armoring had been dissipated, in the true Reichian sense of the term, vital energies which had been locked up or anchored in the muscular hypertension, found their own kind of outlet. Someone long ago said man is a religious animal. The release of these bio-energies brought with them the confirmation of this statement. Some had never before been religious in their lives—others had been raised in the formal religions of today but had become wholly disenchanted, rebelling harshly against them. After thus rejecting the faith of their childhood, suddenly they found themselves developing new and fascinating insights into those early faiths. Even the old prayer and hymns once memorized by rote gradually became alive and revealed new meanings and new stirrings within. They learned spontaneously to pray.

It was not learned in any ordinary sense. And it most assuredly was not something they acquired from me. It was a hard and fast rule of mine never to talk to patients about my metaphysical or occult faith. Most never knew I had written about the subject. Only if they had previously encountered my writings did I acknowledge with some hesitation an interest in these matters. Even then it was sparing, a begrudging acknowledgement—deliberately adopted so that their own growth and development would not be prejudicially affected by me.

So it was all the more gratifying and exciting when, as therapy progressed and their own energies were released, their own native "religious" sense began to emerge. It introduced them to an entirely new way of life, of thinking and feeling and aspiring. It is with all this in mind, that this book is offered—sincerely hoping that the general reader too may find his own path to the heights of attainment. That he too may discover God (whatever he may understand by this), or the Universal Life Energy, in ways that are peculiar and special to him.

My best wishes and blessings, for whatever they may be worth, go forth with this hope.

May 11, 1982
Arizona

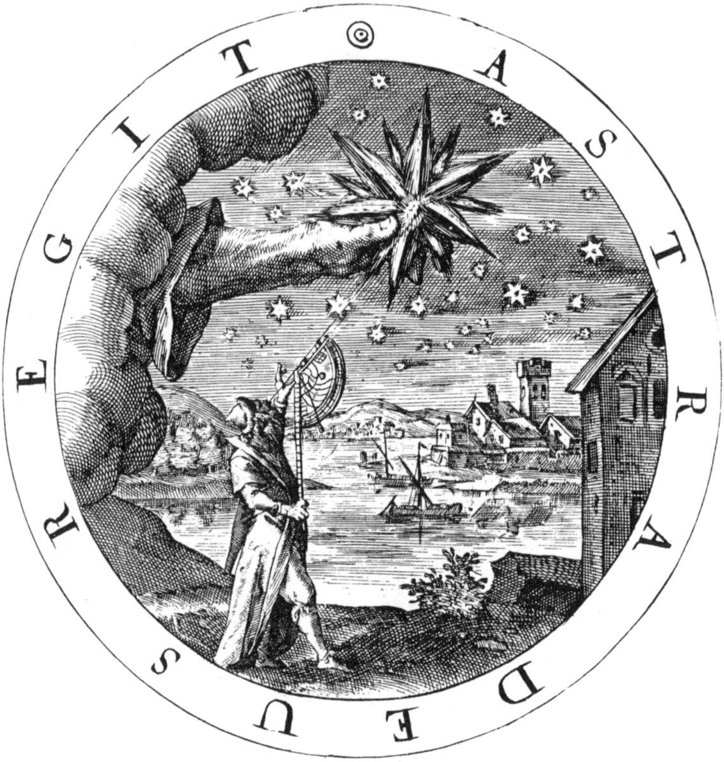
ASTRA DEUS REGIT

Chapter One

A Scientific Approach to Metaphysics

I want to present a new point of view here, that is psychological rather than metaphysical. A scientific approach is possible in at least the primary concepts of metaphysical study. It may well be that if such a scientific attitude can be adopted so that certain states of mind can be induced at will by a psychological technique, we may be able to confer some degree of scientific and popular recognition on metaphysics. The method I am about to delineate here will accomplish precisely this. It is divided for the sake of convenience into two parts. The first deals with relaxation proper. It delineates a technique by means of which the body may achieve a state of such thorough repose that it fades out completely from view. The mind is thus left free to do whatever it wishes. The second will teach the student, by pursuing the same psychological method, how his mind may be trained and educated to dwell successfully on spiritual truths best suited to benefit him.

Moreover, the method possesses this additional advantage. All the metaphysical systems maintain that the mind is able to control the body and its manifold functions—and in fact to affect the entire phenomenal world. To prove this is to manifest successful "demonstrations" of the divine power. The method indicated in succeeding pages will prove to the metaphysical novice that by means of evolving mental pictures, he can himself induce a variety of physiological changes in his body. With this acquired ability, a quiet confidence based upon experience will come to him, an assurance that now he will be able to succeed in "demonstrating" metaphysically his ability to conquer and transcend physical and mental circumstances of every kind.

For the first few attempts at relaxing, it is ideal to work with another person whom you know. The whole function of this second person is merely to make you aware of your own bodily tensions. He has no other role than to call your attention to hypertonic physiological states. These, when called to your attention, tend automatically to fall away—if not wholly, then at least in part. The mere fact that you become aware of them gives you some degree of control over them, and freedom from them. This other person is not absolutely necessary. He is simply an aid—and if it is not convenient, or should it prove impossible to enlist the services of such a friend, this section of my description may be glossed over. For the sake of convenience, let me call the person to be relaxed the subject. The assistant who is going to make the subject aware of his tensions, we will call the teacher. This is simply for the purpose of making clear the instruction to be given.

The subject is to lie down on his back on any hard surface, or on a bed with a hard mattress, or on a table covered by a blanket. A well-carpeted floor has been known to be very satisfactory. Only the head is permitted to rest on a small cushion.

A hard surface seems preferable because immediately the subject is confronted by his tensions. Either he must get up because he feels so uncomfortable—or else he must relax. The choice is clear; there is no alternative. The idea is to let the hard surface support the body. Too often, when lying down, we remain fully tensed when we should permit the muscles to loosen up entirely. Thus we support our bodies by too great tonicity, instead of letting go. The employment of a hard surface will make the individual realize in what way he tenses himself. Having realized this, he will more easily be able to let himself go. Ernest Wilson tells a lovely little story in his *Adventures in Prosperity* that perfectly illustrates the idea. "Once, as a lad, the writer boarded a street car with a heavy suitcase. The car was crowded, and he was obliged to stand. The suitcase seemed to grow heavier and heavier. He shifted it from one hand to the other, and then used both. Finally, a kindly man turned to him, and said, 'Let the world hold it up, Sonny, and rest yourself.' The thought is an old one. It has been told with many variations by many persons."

So also, in relaxing, the student must come to feel that the hard surface is there really to support the body. He must not merely lie on it, but he must give himself wholly up to it. If, after a little practice, he can learn to let himself go, and give himself up for rest on this hard surface, he will have accomplished a miracle that can have far-reaching effects on his life. That is the advantage of learning what is admittedly a purely artificial technique of relaxation. In this way he can learn to relax. And once able to do that, he will find that the faculty acquired will extend into every situation that life may bring. He will be able to relax to life, to "sit loose" to it. Acceptance is probably the most difficult lesson we have to learn. Relaxation is the key to it.

A few deep sighs will prove of inestimable value—the sort of sigh that you would make if, after climbing a steep hill carrying a large and heavy knapsack, you had reached the top and had thrown the sack onto the ground. Your sense of relief would be so marked, and the fatigue so evident, that immediately sighs of relief from effort and from the burden of the sack would be heaved. This will cause some rudimentary relaxation of the diaphragm—a thick, powerful, dome-shaped muscle separating the thoracic from the abdominal cavities. As the diaphragm tends to relax so also will much of the abdomen and chest.

The subject should lie quietly for a couple of minutes, observing himself closely throughout. It will train him in the art of observation and introspection. He must become familiar with the body and its tensions, and learn to notice what the body feels like. Most of us in reality have never had any true awareness of the body at all—except as a heavy burden or grave problem. After some while, the subject will be surprised to realize what a good friend and faithful loyal servant it can turn out to be. So watch yourself and your body. Be keenly observant of all the physiological alterations that ensue, with the psychological changes that are bound to follow. It will prove the introduction into an entirely new world.

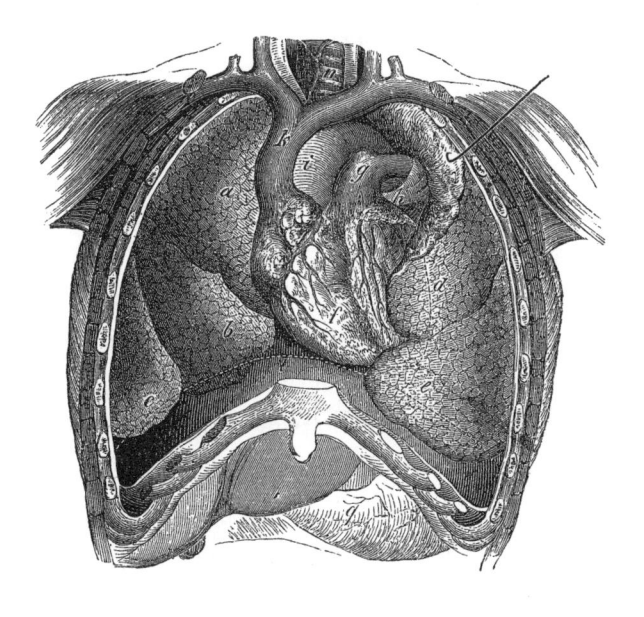

By these means you will come to watch yourself from the inside in preparation to redirecting the mind within, to discover "the secret place of the Most High," the "kingdom of heaven" within the "Temple of the Holy Ghost."

Now we have to consider the role of the teacher. The subject lies down on the hard surface of table or floor, with eyes closed, trying to watch himself and his varied reactions. He will shortly discover that he is totally unable to achieve relaxation. The teacher is now to raise the legs by the heels, one at a time, just a few inches off the surface and let them drop. As a rule, the subject will come to realize that the legs do not drop by themselves—passively. He discovers that involuntarily he holds them up by muscular effort and puts them down the same way. The legs are gripped by an involuntary habit of muscular tension which, because of his unconsciousness of that fact, he has never been able to eliminate. The teacher should raise the leg, but before letting it drop, place one hand under the knee. If the unsupported lower leg does not fall to the surface, it is evident that the unconscious tensions of the leg muscles prevent the fall. The subject must try to remember that he must not force the leg down. It must drop by its own inherent weight, which will occur as soon as he becomes aware of the fact that the teacher is only holding the thigh at the knee, under the popliteal space, and that the leg is not supported in any way. Both legs should be handled in exactly the same way—first separately, and then together.

A great deal of repetition will be found necessary in order to impress upon the subject's consciousness this one fact concerning unconscious or involuntary muscular tensions. Unconsciously the muscles are kept in a tense state, despite the fact that they are not actively being used. An enormous amount of energy is thus being wasted—an amount moreover which can be measured and tested by a basal metabolism respirometer. Apart from all other considerations, this energy wastage alone would prove to be an important reason demanding the induction of adequate relaxation. When once the idea has struck home, the teacher can proceed in a slightly new direction. Let him raise both legs at once—by slipping one hand under the ankles. Only a few inches will be found necessary. When the other hand is slipped under the knees, the hand under the ankles should be removed. This will permit both legs to drop, providing the musculature is in a relaxed state, otherwise the subject will discover the amusing phenomenon of the legs being fixed in midair. Now let him hold the ankles together with one hand, and taking away the supporting hand from beneath the knees, try gently to separate, only slightly, the knees. If the subject is capable of relaxing, each knee will fall outwards. Usually, there is great resistance at the beginning to this relaxation of the adductor muscles of the thighs—especially in girls and women who, for the sake of the experiment, would do well to wear slacks or beach pajamas. I always demand such attire on the part of my female subjects when engaging in a public demonstration of the art and principles of relaxation. Frequent repetition of these principles is necessary until the neurological impulses are able to impress the thigh muscles, to emancipate them into relaxing.

Some considerable attention should be given to both the arms and hands which will usually be found to be extraordinarily tense. The teacher should wriggle the arm a little, rather as one might shake a snake, or a rope. Sometimes this suffices to relax the arm muscles without further ado. With the elbow resting on the hard surface, held there with one hand, the teacher must now raise the forearm and hand of the subject perpendicular to the table. Then, releasing the forearm, he should watch to see whether the forearm falls readily by itself, whether it remains uplifted at right angles to the arm, or whether it is pushed down by muscular effort. The elbow is next, and should be grasped and handled in much the same way. This relaxes the shoulder joint. A wide range of variations are possible, too complex to describe, though not at all difficult to perform. The alert student will devise his own experiments to determine the degree of hypertonicity, and thus relax the tension. A few hours spent in this way during the course of a week or two is not wasting time in the least. The effort will have been invaluable and will prove so later when he attempts meditation and the metaphysical treatments we are really concerned with.

The shoulders can also be assisted to relax by the teacher slipping both hands under one shoulder of the subject, and lifting it slightly, then letting it drop back on the surface. Repeat with the other shoulder. The body should drop heavily, and the head should wag quite freely on the neck. Usually at this time, the subject quite spontaneously will heave a sigh or two indicative of a relaxation that slowly is deepening and becoming more profound. The teacher will be able to see innumerable signs of impending relaxation. Lines on the face and forehead will show signs of disappearing, the respiration becomes fuller and deeper and slower, and the entire body will be seen to sag down more and more upon the surface.

The task of the teacher is next to probe gently with his fingers into the abdominal muscles adjacent to the hip bones. Slight pressure is enough, usually being adequate to elicit strong spasmodic movements of resistance from the powerful abdominal muscles. Maintain the pressure for a few seconds first on the one side and then on the other until the muscles cease their reflex resistance and remain relaxed, becoming softer and softer, in spite of the persistent pressure. If the muscles relax no pain or sensitiveness should be elicited. Pain may be felt only if the subject is fighting the finger probing by increasing the tonicity of the external and

A Scientific Approach to Metaphysics

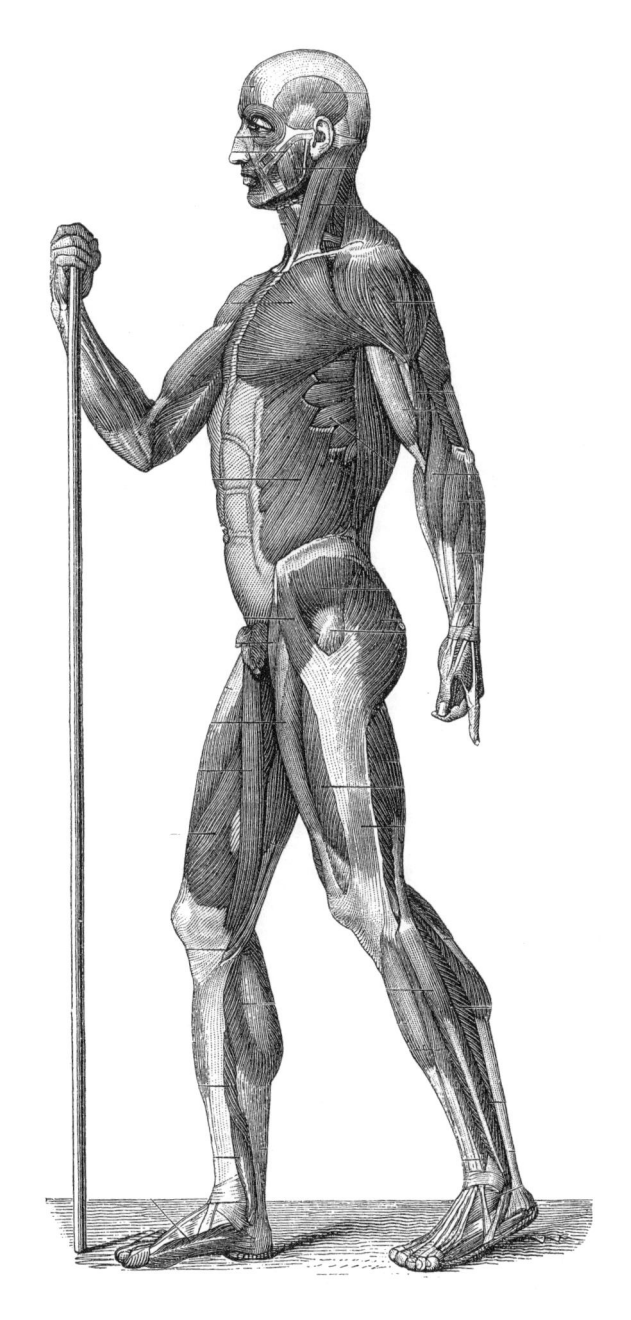

internal oblique and transverse abdominal muscles. Slight pressure should be exerted upon the chest, front and sides, in order to convey to the subject some notion of the elasticity of the thoracic cage. Different lobes of the lungs can be persuaded into specific activity by these pressures, and definite thoracic muscles relaxed.

To complete his phase of the relaxing work, nothing remains for the teacher to do now except very easily and gently to lift the head several times from the surface and let it fall back on the cushion. By the time this procedure has been followed through at least a couple of times, the student will feel considerably more relaxed than he has for ages. At this juncture, he can wholly dispense with the teacher and carry on independently of any outside help. Now he is on his own, and from then on he really begins to learn the fine art of relaxation.

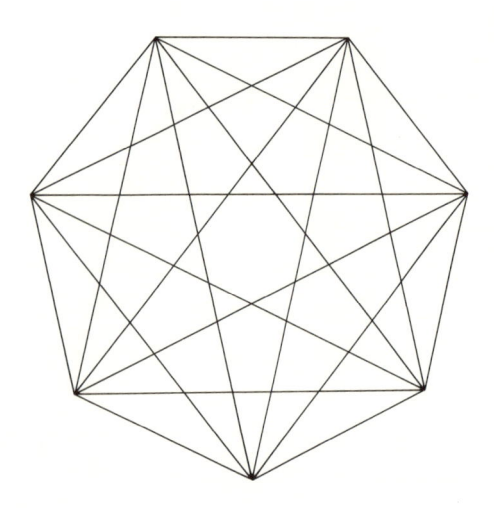

Chapter Two

Perfect Relaxation

Having become aware of the principal gross tensions, and dispensed with the assistant, the student may now proceed with the real technique for the induction of perfect relaxation. It is this which bears relation to metaphysical effort. Its rationale is based upon a very simple fact which everyone knows. If you have been dreaming that you are running down a street with someone in hot pursuit, you are likely to wake up feeling very breathless, a little frightened, and with a racing heart and rapid respiration. The dream consists of a series of psycho-motor stimuli, so dynamic in nature, as to demand translation into visible and even measurable physiological reactions. In much the same way, if you sat down and quite consciously began thinking of such a dream, meditating intently upon its action, a similar phenomenon would occur within a very short time. Ideas retained in consciousness tend to discharge themselves into the body. This is a fundamental physio-psychological fact.

 A favorite device of mine for proving that psychological states and mental images do produce immediate physical results, is to ask a student to sit down, breathing deeply until he feels quiet, and then relaxed. Then, without imparting my motive, I ask him to build up in his mind a series of mental pictures. For example, he may be asked to visualize a beautiful, golden sandy beach. He is lying on the sand, basking in the warm sunshine, perfectly relaxed and contented. So warm does he become—it is a hot midsummer's day—that he is obliged to enter the ocean for a swim, to cool off. Getting up from the sand, and stretching vigorously, he sees himself imaginatively make a running leap for the water, dives in, and begins swimming rapidly through the surf and breakers out to a hundred yard point in the sea. He floats there for a few minutes on his back. Having regained his wind and composure, he swims back to the beach as rapidly as possible—just as quickly as though he were entered for a swimming competition. He gets back to the shore, relaxes on the sand, and lets go.

All this time I have been keenly observing the student's respiration, pulse and temperature. All undergo a rapid cycle of changes. They decline, increase and decrease—depending upon the activity that he imagines himself to engage in. These I record on a chart. When he opens his eyes, after the termination of this psychological experiment, he is able to read the chart and graph that I have drawn as tangible evidence of his mental gymnastics. This is concrete evidence that is highly convincing, giving the student vast assurance in the validity of the relaxation technique that follows.

If the psychological states are able, demonstrably, to produce immediate reactions in the psycho-somatic system, then we can usefully employ mental pictures in order consciously to induce a state of relaxation preliminary to metaphysical treatment. I consider the relaxation state of paramount importance because by this means we are able to acquire a state of consciousness in which there is no trace of physical, somatic elements whatsoever. It is a state of pure consciousness, without any other determinants.

The pictures useful for inducing a relaxation of neuromuscular hypertonicity are those that relate to the blood. We know scientifically that if vascular congestion occurs in any part of the body, at least two phenomena occur. First, there is increased thermogenesis. Secondly, there is a relaxation of the unstriped arterial muscles which widen the lumen or caliber of the blood vessels. Hence, if we can produce artificial vascularization of any tissue, we will develop an inner warmth, followed by a relaxing of the surrounding hypertension in that area. Now, to think of any part of the body is immediately to increase locally the blood supply. If you sat down, held out your hand, and gazed at your thumb for several seconds, after a while there will be increased sensation there, as though it had become engorged. This experiment can be applied to any part of the body.

What is proposed then, is for the student to consider in his imagination every part of the body—from brain to the tips of the toes. There is no escape from body here, no running away from all that the body implies. It is to be faced starkly in all its nakedness, and the physical and psychic tensions exposed, subjected to treatment on a sound physiological basis, and thus overcome. No intricate knowledge of anatomy is really necessary. On the other hand, if the student has been taught the broad generalities relating to the anatomy and physiology of the bodily mechanism he will find that knowledge most useful.

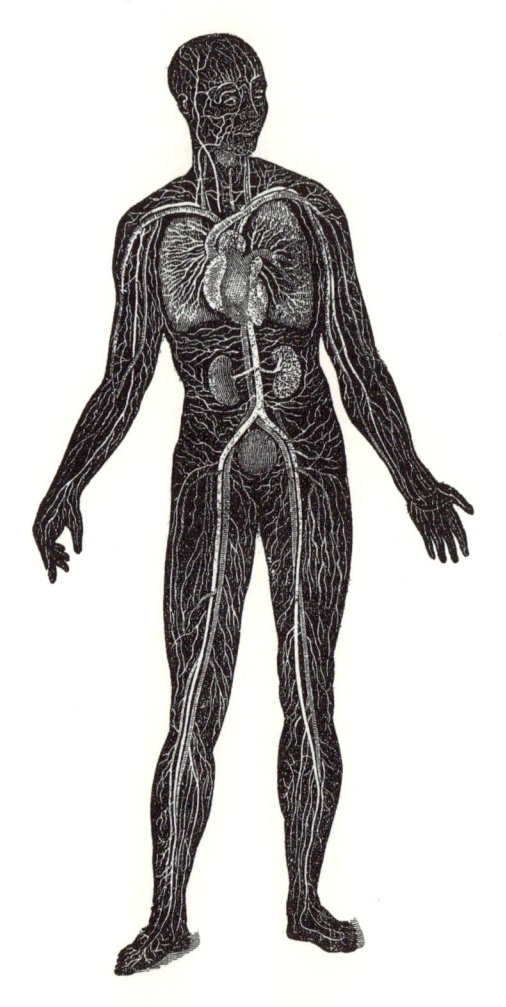

First of all, while lying on the back, a pillow should be slipped under the knees so that they are raised some few

Perfect Relaxation

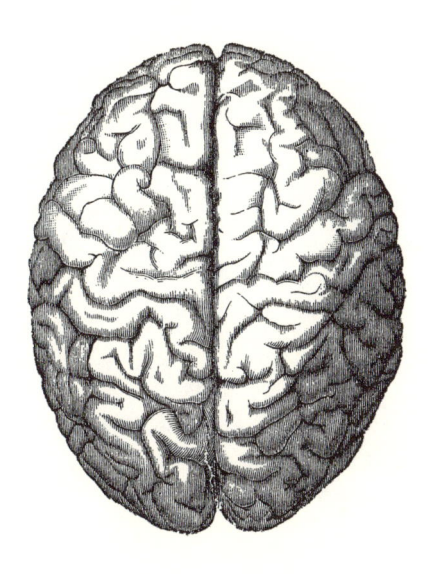

inches. This tends to induce a mechanical relaxation of the spine and the powerful muscles attached to the vertebrae. Let him cross one ankle over another, the heels resting on the hard surface, and fold the hands over the abdomen by interlacing the fingers. Consider the brain now by visualizing it in the skull. Everyone has seen pictures of the cerebrum, so this will not be too difficult. Consider the brain to be a mass of white and grey nerve substance, divided into a right and left hemisphere, with a little bulb at the back, the cerebellum. The entire surface of these structures is marked by numbers of lobes, convolutions and depressions or sulci. Visualize the brain clearly if you can, and feel it with the imagination. Try to feel that this brain, normally white and grey in color, becomes pinkish in hue as you think of it, automatically directing an increased blood supply to its structures. Maintain this visualization for about a minute. By that time, there should certainly be some kind of sensation there—subjective sensations of warmth, and a curious feeling which can only be described by tingling. This is not only subjective, for the physical phenomena can be checked by medical diagnostic instruments. When this is achieved, you can descend a little bit with your visualizations to other organs of the body.

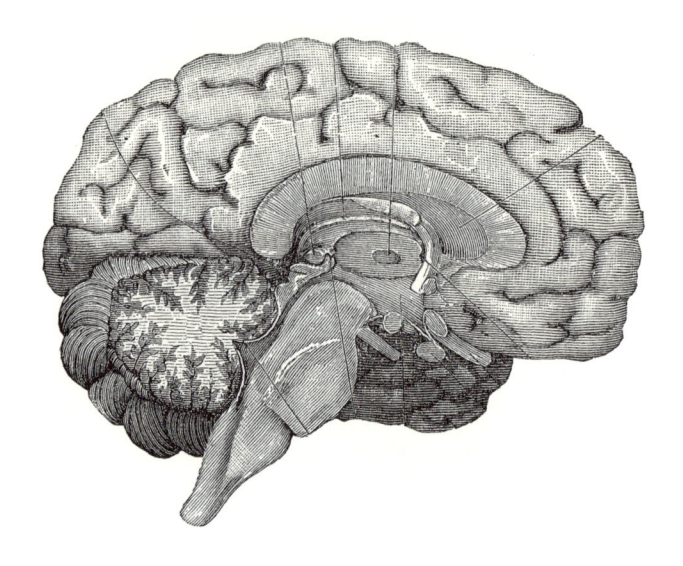

During the process of relaxing, when all the tissues are being bathed in blood, various sensations arise which can most easily and best be described as a tingling. It is akin to the so-called pins and needles sensation which is felt when circulation is being restored to a limb, after a temporary partial blocking by pressure of some one of the blood-vessels. Charles Fillmore, the Unity leader, experienced similar sensations during the course of his long meditations. When he was still tubercular, and practiced reflection on the presence

Perfect Relaxation

and healing power of God, he would become aware of electric sensations in his extremities—sensations of aliveness, of tingling. These would be considerably enhanced if his attention was focussed on special localities or areas of the body. He believed that by turning his attention God-wards, his whole body became healed and regenerated. The result was that the tubercular infection was checked, and he lived for many years in active service on behalf of the Unity School. Relaxing the body thoroughly by these methods, and experiencing the sensation of relaxation fully, will be found to act as a distinct stimulus to the maintenance and recovery of perfect health.

Imagine next that the blood, which has been warming and so relaxing the brain, pours downwards from the frontal portions of the cerebrum into the forehead, the eyes and the temples. Go through a similar procedure as described above, until you obtain that inner sense of warmth, tingling, and relaxation. They are quite unmistakable sensations, and are certain signs of the induction of a local release of tension. Pass in contemplation downwards to the ears, thinking also of the middle and inner ear with its intricate mechanism, the cheeks of the face and the nose. Pause until the appropriate reactions and sensations are noted clearly in consciousness.

Meantime, should the attention wander away to the events of the day, business worries, domestic problems, or anything else, do not be angry or annoyed. Wait quietly for a few seconds and quite gently bring the attention back to consideration of the organ in question. Above all, do not let annoyance or mental tension arise. Deal with the problem very simply and directly. The mind is bound to wander at the beginning. It requires training and re-education. That takes time. Just wait a moment or two should the attention falter, then turn the mind back towards the production of hyperaemia in the local area. Bring the blood in your imagination to the lips, the mouth, the gums of the teeth, and the tongue, the chin and the angles of the jaw.

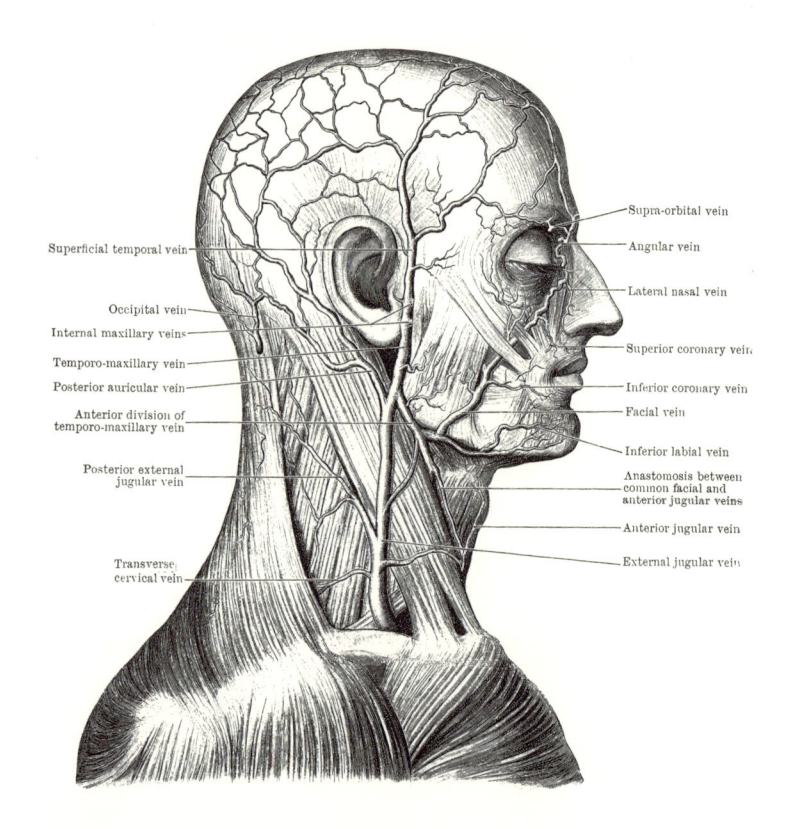

This procedure having been applied to the whole head, including the back of the head, you should pause for a little while to become completely aware of the sensations involved.

Perfect Relaxation

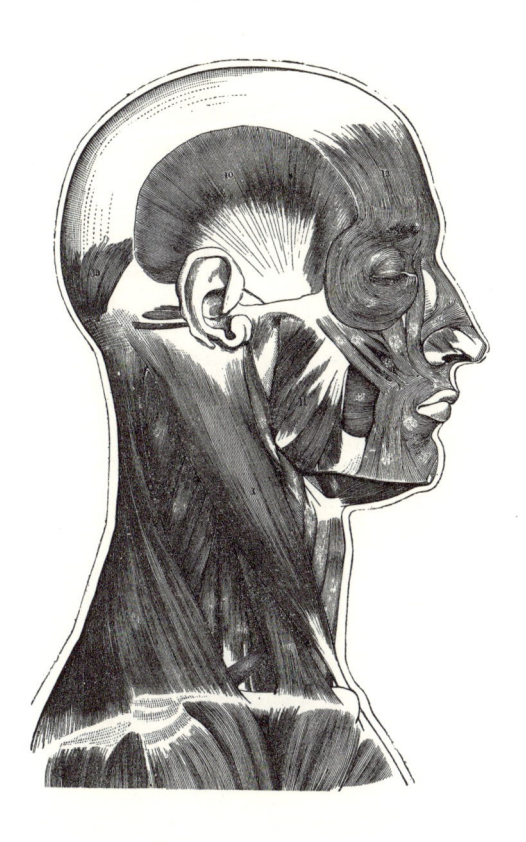

Also note that the entire body should have begun to lose its tensions, for since the brain is the neurological center of the whole psycho-somatic organism, as it relaxes so also will all other subsidiary parts. The student who knows his neuro-anatomy can apply this technique to a consideration of the area about the fourth ventricle and the medulla, for here are important reflex centers, which include the respiratory, cardiac and thermogenetic centers, as well as the nerve roots of the last three cranial nerves so intimately connected with the functions of the viscera.

The neck is the next area to be considered. The student should visualize the windpipe, or the pharynx and larynx and trachea. The muscles and glands in the front, sides, and back of the neck should be imagined as being bathed in blood, being gently warmed by its heat, and thus being made to relax. As the hypertonicity begins to loosen, pass the attention to the powerful muscles of the shoulders and shoulder joints. Pay great attention to these, for they are unusually tense in most modern people. Hypertension and sensitivity of the trapezium are one of the characteristic symbols of the city dweller, one of the prices we pay for modern life—and some people think a rather exorbitant one.

Let the attention slowly wander from the shoulders down the arm to the elbow, forearm, wrist, hand and fingers, dwelling for a minute or so on each part, feeling the sensation of warmth and tingling there, telling each part with definiteness to relax. Return in the imagination once more to the shoulders. Visualize the entire thoracic cage. This consists of the ribs connected to the sternum or breast bone in front, and to the spine at the back, separated from the abdominal cavity below by the diaphragm. Within this chest box are several large and important organs—the bronchi, lungs, heart, and the great arteries and veins leading to and from it. Powerful muscles lie between the ribs to aid the respiratory function. Just make a simple picture of this box which the thorax is, and begin to feel that slowly the blood pours into every artery, arteriole and capillary. The muscles which comprise the walls of these vessels relax, enabling them to convey larger quantities of blood than before. Because of this increased blood supply, a greater warmth is being generated in the thorax, resulting in a generally diffused sense of relaxation.

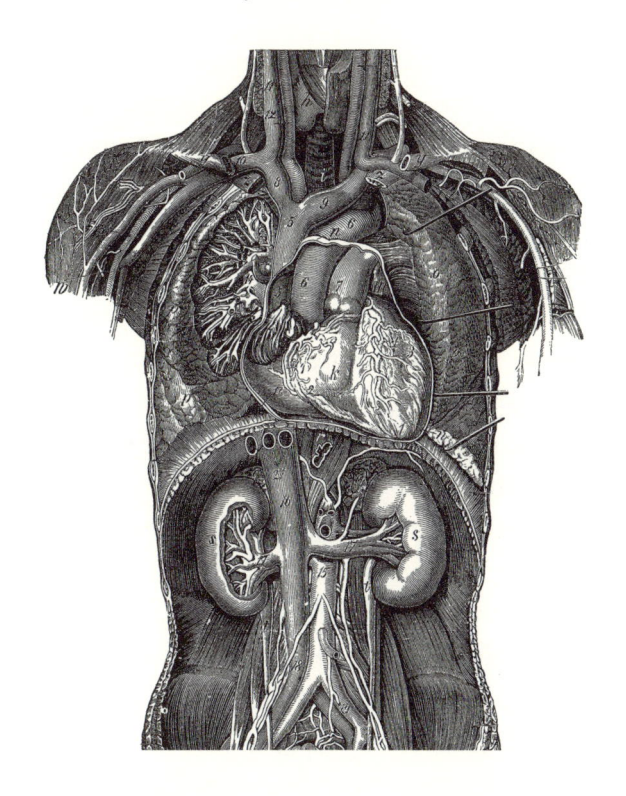

So far as the abdomen and pelvis is concerned a similar technique is to be followed, thinking of the large area which includes the individual organs that you know to be there. Feel the warm descent of the blood, and experience fully the sensation of aliveness that the thinking about those parts produces. As you practice you will at first become increasingly conscious of each bodily section, becoming aware of each separate organ rather as one does of each tooth during an acute toothache. This sensation is succeeded by a complete cessation of sensory awareness. The relaxed portion, formerly standing out so clearly to consciousness, will fade utterly from sight. Eventually, consciousness of the body as a whole vanishes entirely, and a deep and abiding serenity and stillness remains.

Having completed the irrigation of the pelvic area, imagine the life-stream of blood dividing into two powerful rivers, each sweeping down one hip and thigh. Consider the thigh as far down as the knee-cap, in a manner similar to that applied to all other portions of the body until you become aware of the warmth and relaxing of the muscles. Then pass downwards with the mind to the ankle, and finally to the tips of the toes.

Become fully aware of each minute part of the body becoming absolutely flooded by the blood-stream, which enables it to undergo this needed release from hypertensiveness. The entire process, from head to toe, should take not less than half an hour at first. More would be more satisfactory. As time goes on, less time will be necessary to induce relaxation, until finally the mere wish or thought to relax will spontaneously induce all muscles and tissue everywhere in the body to relax their ordinary tension. Skill is the important factor, and skill is achieved by practice and constant repetition.

The sense of ease and relief from bodily tension is likely to become so intense that the student may fall asleep. This result should not be combated, for it will pass away in a short while. It seems that most of us, over long periods of time, have so thoroughly identified ourselves with bodily activity

Perfect Relaxation

that when finally such activity ceases, there is nothing for the mind to attach itself to. Therefore its activity too undergoes an eclipse, sleep ensuing as the logical result. This refreshing sleep of relaxation should not be interfered with. It is just as well for the student to let sleep come as he relaxes. In a short time, as he becomes more and more expert in irrigating each bodily organ and relaxing it, he will learn to separate himself in consciousness from his body. So that when eventually the body does relax and enter the sleep state, he as a mind will remain alert and wide awake. The tendency to slip into sleep will disappear. His mind will be totally distinct and differentiated from the body and its functions.

A strange phenomenon usually arises at this juncture. So completely does the body relax, that all body consciousness disappears. One is simply not aware that there is such a thing as a body. One is a mind only—conscious and thinking, aware of self and its ideas. But as for body—there is no body. No attempt has been made to deny the material body, or to question philosophically its existence or validity. This is a scientific observation, as valid as any objective observation of any scientific subject. This result occurs spontaneously. In one sense, it would appear as though the body needs are fulfilled, and the student, in having become fully conscious of the body now lets it descend into complete unconsciousness to function perfectly without psychological interference. This alone has a therapeutic affect.

In doing this, the mind is given a tremendous impetus towards freedom. No longer is it held back from meditation and prayer because of physical disturbances. No longer will physical sensations or pain stimulate currents of psychological activities which are prone to interfere with the higher activities of the mind and spirit. The mind feels sublimely released, able to concentrate all its energies upon the work at hand. And the sense of freedom from body awareness is so intense as almost to amount to a feeling of ecstasy, of real bliss. The student will discover for himself, for the first time in his life maybe, the real capacity of the mind to function without hindrance, without the relentless awareness of the physical limitations that formerly dogged his footsteps. And this is such a staggering acquisition as to reflect itself automatically into his personality. Poise and self-assurance seem to follow from such a psychological and spiritual achievement. The very relaxation of the body, which in itself seems to be related to unconscious states of the mind, tends to dissolve those psychic conflicts which were the etiological factors in the production of psycho-somatic tensions and disease states. Even the people about one, the environment itself, will soon come to reflect these changes that the relaxation technique produces.

Chapter Three

God's Presence and Relaxation

To be able to acquire a relaxed state of both body and mind is an asset that will prove invaluable in hosts of circumstances arising in the ordinary course of living. Not only so, but the student will be in possession of a psychological method of influencing beneficently his body, a technique capable of extension in manifold directions. Pain can often be relieved by resort to this method. Congestion or cold in any area can be eliminated by this imaginative moving of the blood from head to foot.

But this is only the least part of the full picture that is important. The more interesting extension, as I have suggested, is its application to metaphysical technique and prayer treatments. The student will have learned infallibly that he can, by meditating upon the different localities of his body, completely eliminate the body as a whole from his consciousness as an irritant and as a deterrent to spiritual activity. But now he can begin to make application of the method to bring about spiritual activity, not merely to eradicate deterrents to it. He will know that his mind has powers of its own which were previously unsuspected—powers which produce immediate effects upon the body. And this is invaluable knowledge giving him confidence and assurance in dealing with the higher facets of metaphysical application.

Certain conventions of visual thought, or imaginative artifices are required of the student in this advanced technique. If his efforts are moving in the direction of becoming God-conscious, God-saturated, and capable of practicing constantly the realization of the presence of God, he must use his mind in peculiar, yet definite ways to achieve that end. For this purpose, my usual practice is once more to ask the student to bear with me, and to apply his visual imaginative powers to conceiving of himself and his body in certain ways. He is asked to consider the well-known fact that the skin all over his body is perforated by thousands of minute holes called pores. Moreover, every organ in his body, being composed of cells of different types, likewise is perforated by countless intercellular spaces, interstices of various sizes. In other words, by a contemplation of this anatomical fact, he will begin to realize that the concept of physical solidity and impermeability is merely a convenient concept. It is one, which for our purpose, has not a great deal of validity.

The realization of the conclusions here can be enhanced tremendously by carrying the argument still further. Each cell, it must be remembered, is a protoplasmic structure, composed of numbers of highly complex molecules. Each molecule, upon chemical analysis, is seen to be composed of many elements—carbon, oxygen, hydrogen, nitrogen, potas-

God's Presence and Relaxation

sium, sulfur, iron, and so forth. The structure of the molecule includes large numbers of atoms bound together in certain activity patterns. Likewise these atoms may be broken down and realized to be composed of electrons and protons, positive and negative electric charges, or light-waves, knit into units according to known electro-magnetic and physical laws. In reality, however, the entire body is immaterial in structure and essence, being composed exclusively of charges of electricity and waves of light. The mere contemplation of such scientific facts will go far towards establishing firm mental control of physiological function, relaxing the body as a preparatory means of eliminating it as a disturbing factor to meditation.

The student can carry this relation still further by recalling all the references, for example, in the Bible with regard to Light and its nature. Jesus said "I am the light of the world," and in the gospel of St. John we read "There was the true light, even the light which lighteth every man, coming into the world." And mystics everywhere all over the world, no matter in what age or race they have lived, have experienced the realization of God's presence in terms of light and ecstasy. They feel and see blazes of brilliant light and color. Everything becomes light. They realize themselves to live in a light world. Hence, the student, in realizing that his body is made up of waves of light may, by remembering all these facts, come to realize that even his body is God, made up of God's substance which is light, and that at no time is there ever any kind of separateness between him and the supreme source of all.

But let us return to the imaginative concept of the skin being perforated by numbers of holes, of pores. The student should be lying on his back, in the formal relaxation position. Later, when considerable skill is obtained, he will not need to recline in this or any other special way. Relaxation will occur so immediately that it can be induced anywhere, at any time, merely by willing it to occur, by thinking of it. But for the initial purpose of mastering the technique he should recline, with closed eyes in order to shut out external sensory impressions. Lying down, then, relaxed, imagine the skin on the cheeks of the face, feeling that the pores in the skin are stretched wide open, large, yawning, precipices and gulfs on the face. A few seconds' work will usually suffice—especially if he has previously followed the former relaxing technique, by means of which the body will respond readily to the thought. Then extend this idea to the skin on the forehead, nose and entire face. Include also the scalp and the back of the head. Contemplate, in each area, that no longer is the skin impermeable and non-porous, but that it is composed of more holes that tissue. In fact, the symbol of a woman's hair-net will perfectly convey the idea to be grasped.

The entire body should be thought of in this way, following the surface of the skin downwards from the head, neck, shoulders and arms, thorax, pelvis and abdomen, thighs, legs and feet. He should consider every part, coming to realize that the membrane which surrounds the organs of the body, holding it together as a limiting membrane, has lost its density and impermeability and is actually a series of holes loosely knit together by a net-like tissue. Reaching the toes and soles of the feet, he should pause temporarily to acquire the full sensation of the stretching of the pores—a completely unmistakable sensation.

This sensation acquired, now let him return to reflection of the head once more. But this time, his imagination will extend interiorly rather than externally. He should consider the brain, not as in the preliminary relaxation technique with a view to vascularizing its neurological tissue, but in order to arrive at the feeling that it has become full of holes. The student should try to acquire the sensation that the interstices between the cells are becoming greater, and that the brain is, in a word, becoming sponge-like. If he can consider a sponge, he will have succeeded in realizing what I am attempting to describe by feeling that the substance of the brain is similarly constructed. This may take some little time, but once obtained it can be induced again with the greatest of ease.

This sponge feeling should now be applied to all organs of the body. Deal with the head first of all. Feel, in turn, that the brain, the eyes, the nose, the ears, all the viscera of the head are sponge-like, replacing the solid tissue. Then continue with the neck, imagining that the cervical vertebrae of the spine, the neck muscles and flesh, larynx, esophagus and glands—in fact, visualizing that the whole neck has become like a sponge, full of holes. Apply a similar technique to the shoulders and arms. Visualize that bone, as well as muscles and tendons and ligaments, respond to exactly the same image. The thorax with its adnexia of lungs, heart, bloodvessels, etc. likewise comprises a large sponge. The abdomen and pelvis, thighs and legs also disappear save as they are felt to be masses of holes bound into an integrated whole.

It is important that this realization be obtained fully before he continues. It is not so difficult, and most people can obtain it within a very short period of time. The sensations attending the realization are distinctive, and cannot be mistaken for any other bodily reaction. Rarely have I had any failures with the many people whom I have taught in a professional capacity. But once the faculty is acquired of feeling, during the meditation, that the body is a sponge and is full of holes, this sensation can be developed in a highly practical way. The student should try to remember the idea of Berkeleyan philosophy that sensation tells us not of material objects, but of divine ideas retained in the universal mind of God—this will enable him to transcend the plane of mere technique.

God's Presence and Relaxation

Now if the body is full of perforations, the student should consider that since the atmosphere encloses him at every moment during the day, the now absolutely permeable body offers no impediment whatsoever to the entrance of air. In fact, so far from resisting the flow of air through his body, he knows that the atmosphere must literally rush and course through these myriads of holes which he now feels his body to be. As he reclines, fully relaxed, let him imagine that the atmosphere immediately above him pours through his body, pushing downwards from the ceiling. He may combine this with the rhythm of his breathing. As he breathes in, let him realize that the air saturates the sponge that is his body, pouring into him from above, from head to toe. With the exhalation of breath, the air leaves his porous body, making its exit all the way along the back of his head, the back of his trunk, thighs and legs. Continue this thought for some several seconds, until the feeling of the permeability of the body to the atmosphere grows. Let the student vary the exercise, first by imagining that he breathes in through the holes in the soles of his feet, the air rushing vigorously along the whole course of his body, and exhaling through the crown of his head— and vice versa. Then that the atmosphere rises up from beneath him, passing out through him in front to rise to the ceiling above.

These are simply a series of imaginative concepts which have the effect of first relaxing the body and mind, and at the same time preparing the trained mind to consider spiritual truths. The spiritual fact to be considered is the primordial relationship existing between air and spirit. In all primitive languages, the word for air is the same as that for spirit and mind. Both are life and the carriers of life. Without air there can be no manifestation of life.

Let the student therefore begin to consider mentally the idea that this air rushing through his body so completely open to its influx and offering no impediment or barrier—this air is the divine Spirit, it is the universal life which animates all created things. This air is God who, so all the metaphysical systems teach, is an omnipresent, infinite, omnipotent principle. Spirit is everywhere at all times, and there is no part of space which is exempt from its presence. God is all powerful; we cannot conceive of any competing or opposing force. Nor can we conceive that He should have any limitations of any kind that our minds can conceive of. He is divine wisdom and truth, and all our knowledge and learning is but an infinitesimal fragment of the omniscience of the universal Spirit. He, likewise, is all-love, an all embracing love that is so keen and intense that those men who touch that love in their consciousness, rave of the ineffable ecstasy and bliss that came in their realization. All these qualities belong to God, and these are those characteristics that the student should contemplate as he begins to consider the relationship with Spirit and air—the air that rushes through his body and mind.

By imagining the air to saturate the completely porous and permeable body, we are in reality arriving at a high consciousness of the ever-presence and power of God. God pervades every minute cell of the body. No atom, no minute particle anywhere in this body can possibly be free of the power and substance and intelligence and love that God is. All the knowledge of metaphysics that the student has acquired may now be thrown with the utmost intensity and concentration into the meditation, with the complete assurance and knowledge that he has achieved success. He has already gained confidence in the efficacy of his mind by having applied himself to the techniques previously described. The practice of the presence of God is only an extension of it. A true realization of God's infinite nature may thus be divined, in such a way that no violence is done either to body or to mind. All parts of man are fulfilled, justified without unnatural denial or negligence. Hence the realization obtained of God must be full and complete—a perfect and harmonious identification with divine power and life and love.

Chapter Four

Prayer

A gesture is any kind of motion, physical or mental, that reflects or conveys an inner meaning. It can be a moral intention or merely a passing thought. To be able to make the right gestures at the right time is probably to be able to accomplish what the gesture is intended for. For the thought is there, and either consciously or otherwise thought precedes action. No man in his right mind would make pugilistic gestures to a prize-fighter unless he felt himself capable of making some kind of determined stand or impression with his gesture. Above all, the right gesture implies a definite attitude of mind. It represents a point of view. To have developed a psychological outlook which can evoke or accompany the right gesture must necessarily imply a long anterior discipline or history.

That prayer consists of just such a series of mental and spiritual gestures is an idea at once so fascinating and so fraught with significance that it is possible that the nail has been hit squarely on the head. If God, by definition, is at once infinite, eternal, omnipotent and omniscient, it would seem that there is hardly any need of prayer at all. All our problems would immediately be divinely appreciated and understood without any necessity on our part to express them and ask in prayer for their solution. Prayer gestures in this sense would be worthless and useless. Most prayers are servile petitions, requests for assistance, for solution to problems which we feel we cannot solve by ourselves unaided, and by our human faculties. We feel some power more divine than ourselves is required—a power that possesses supreme knowledge and love and wisdom.

If, however, we have to ask for help of such a God, automatically we express grave doubt as to His wisdom, intelligence and capabilities. By voicing our aspiration and need in prayer, surely we cannot coerce God to answer us and solve our problems. And if we cannot coerce him, the prayer as a mechanism to this end is useless. Prayer as such cannot move God or alter His decisions, change His views, or do anything not formerly conceived by Him. The modern man, mature, and grown to full adult stature, with a well-developed brain and to some extent versed in the sciences, cannot stoop to anything so puerile and primitive as this. He is obliged by his training and his intellectual outlook to reject such an attitude and such a concept of both God and prayer as unworthy of him. His entire integrity would be thoroughly violated by it.

If, however, prayer is conceived as a dynamic gesture on our part to increase awareness of this imminent spiritual principle which abides in nature as well as in our hearts, then the whole matter becomes considerably clearer. It does not offend us, nor cause us to shrink away in disgust. We are not trying through prayer to affect God, to urge him desperately to come to our rescue, and heal us of our ills. Nor do we attempt to cajole Him to fill the void created by poverty, solitude, or economic difficulties of various kinds.

Prayer is a psychological gesture directed towards knowing and realizing the real self which stands in intimate relationship to the whole stream of life and living experience. Through the gesture of prayer, we attempt to turn the mind around. First of all, the habitual orientation of the mind must be changed. We are in a rut, and usually satisfied with the security and quietude of the rut. A true neophobia has been developed. Change becomes a threat to the self, and our whole security seems in jeopardy. Another point of view must be developed, in which the true significance of change in its relationship to security is realized. Moreover, we must realize that we do not attempt to influence God. Quite obviously, He cannot be influenced by us anyway. What we are endeavoring to do through a series of dynamic gestures, is to relax the involuntary tension of the mind, and afterwards to exalt it to a high and noble pitch, to a consciousness of God. As an omnipresent and imminent principle, God is then able to permeate the mind and work through it for our salvation. The difficulties confronting us are then dealt with not merely by ourselves in the normal but impotent frame of mind, but by God and His ever-present wisdom and love and bounty.

The fundamental idea involved in prayer as a technical process is to exalt the human consciousness to a contemplation of the divine function and principle that exists throughout all nature and within ourselves. Normally the functions

Prayer

of our mind are so bound up with all the trivialities both of personality and of the social world, that we are not in the least bit aware of this divine activity constantly proceeding in the hidden depths of the soul. But is just that unconscious divine activity of which we must become conscious, would we remain connected to the vast current of life upon which all things depend. It is the very life of all of us, and cut off from these divine roots we are sterile and barren, as good as dead. Since usually we are not conscious of its presence, a series of powerful mental gestures of one kind or another must be made, having as their object a radical change in the habitual motion of the mind. Such a change induced by means of the dynamic gestures of prayer, can then put us in touch, through an exalted consciousness, with this divine spiritual force which is everywhere present and everywhere active as boundless love and substance and intelligence.

The mere fact that we can express the prayer problem as becoming conscious of something that hitherto was unconscious, brings the entire subject well within the realms of psychological knowledge. If modern man is unable to accept the idea of God in the religious sense as expressed throughout this book, then at least it is possible to conceive of deeper levels of mind, which if understood and realized, would increase the value and worth of life and living. This supreme value of meaning and integration is after all the God idea, whether we call it God or the Unconscious. The whole intent both of Freudian and Jungian psychology is to enhance consciousness, to widen its horizons, to break down this terrible unconsciousness of our true significance which blinds us to the meaning of human relationships and the world. To attempt this task is to investigate all those facets of the dark unconsciousness of our lives, to restore our reliance upon the deeper roots of ourselves—those vital roots of instinct and intuition the knowledge of which we have so sadly lost in our mad rush to become "civilized." Since the deeper levels of our minds are still in process of discovery and understanding, and since we know very little of their significance, we can, for the sake of argument, identify the unknown unconscious with the unknown God. And through specific and definite inner gestures, either of formal psychological understanding or of mystical prayer, we can arrive at an improved perception and inward realization of this unconscious but divine element in life. The use of the word "unconscious" does not imply for one moment that this element is lacking in consciousness. It only means that we are unconscious and totally unaware of its presence and activity.

The great problem has always been—how shall we attain such awareness? We are willing to admit that God may exist—no matter how we define His existence. We also know that we are not conscious of His presence and power, and that we are sick, poor and beset by a dismal host of problems. But how may we become aware of His presence actively stirring within us? In part, the positing of the problem in this way gives some inkling of the nature of the solution. Unaware of God's presence because of the ceaseless movement of the brain, with its preoccupation with the trivialities of everyday life and experience, then it would follow that could we still this constant frittering of mental activity we would be on the

Prayer

way to the greatest discovery of our lives. If we could only achieve an inner serenity and quiet even for a few moments, that would be enough. Possibly in that silence God would talk to us and give us guidance. "Peace, be still!" is certainly a technique of the utmost significance. The cultivation of a period of silence every day would go a very long way in this direction. Not at once will the mind be quieted. Its habits of continual movement and objective thought and concern over things and ideas must slowly be conquered, to be replaced by better habits which will conduce to higher realizations. To become aware of God must imply some species of specialized mental discipline and training, which very few of us have bothered to acquire. God cannot speak through a disorderly mind. That would be akin to pouring good wine into dirty and old bottles. Divine inspiration working through a muddied and ill-disciplined mind would only have the effect of polluting the inspiration, not of cleansing the bottle. It would provide a tremendous potential which would increase the neurotic trends of the mind and energize the pathological residues in us.

To my mind that is why many of the present psychological techniques are so valuable. No matter how one approaches the problem of cleansing the mind, the methods of Jungian or Freudian psychological analysis are pre-eminently successful in that they also establish a relationship between the conscious mind and unconscious psychological states. By these means a great deal of muck that was unsuspected is thrust completely out of the mental sphere. It leaves a cleansed vehicle which is unlikely to suffer or to deteriorate as a result of metaphysical work and enquiry. All too often, the metaphysician achieves occasional spectacular results and demonstrations, only to find after the passage of many years that he has become ill or spiritually impotent, the prey of irrational fears and beliefs which he can scarcely combat. This phenomenon I have witnessed so frequently that today I have no doubt whatsoever of its accuracy. Mary Baker Eddy and her phobia about malicious animal magnetism is a splendid case in point. There are many others equally striking. The psychological techniques provide a mental discipline which is invaluable. And moreover they provide a technique by means of which outmoded attitudes can readily be discarded, and prepare adequately for that revolution of the mind which we seek as the goal of prayer and spiritual endeavor.

Some kind of daily discipline, altogether apart from analysis, is surely required. All metaphysical teachers in some way recognize this, and therefore recommend a daily study period. "Every soul must take time daily for quiet and meditation," wrote Emilie Cady in her *Lessons in Truth*. "In daily meditation lies the secret of power. No one can grow in either spiritual knowledge or power without it. Practice the presence of God just as you would practice music. No one would ever dream of becoming a power in music except by spending some time daily alone with music. Daily meditation alone with God seems, some way, to focus the divine presence within us and to our consciousness."

In this period, the individual prepares himself through the study of a biblical text, or some portion of one of the books describing metaphysical theory and practice. The Bible, all agree as regarding it their basic textbook. Mrs. Eddy's *Science and Health*, Emilie Cady's *Lessons in Truth*, Ernst Homes' *Science of Mind*, Daniel Boone Herring's *Mind Surgery*, Harriet Hale Rix's *Christian Mind Healing*, and Ralph Waldo Trine's *In Tune with the Infinite*, to name a few, are typical instances of other such recommended books. By such specialized reading, the mind becomes acquainted with fundamental concepts which prepare it to dwell for a few minutes in quietness and silence on the idea of the omnipresent God, of the imminent deity indwelling the heart. By itself, the practice of daily turning the mind inward instead of outwards is adequate enough to teach it entirely new habits of thought and ideation. So that, depending upon the student, in a very short while he becomes accustomed to the silence. No longer does it seem a strange and unfamiliar frame of mind. He begins to evaluate it correctly as the state indispensable to successful prayer, where he can aspire to a knowledge of God.

The relaxation technique described in a former chapter will likewise answer very well to his need for a new discipline of mind. Its object specifically is to eliminate, systematically, awareness of externals, enabling the mind to focus inwardly, accustoming it to function by itself without the necessity of external stimuli. Moreover, a silence interiorly is created. It is a kinetic state which, as the student becomes accustomed to it, will reveal what he only previously suspected or knew, the indwelling God.

All techniques are valid and useful, each in its own particular way. Other methods are commonly used. Some people, for example, will use the Lord's prayer when they have

achieved some familiarity with the quiet state created within. In fact, they use it to create for themselves the serenity and quiet and self-assurance they long for. The metaphysical schools have provided their own interpretations of the meaning of this prayer— even their own wordings. Many of these are profound and erudite to a degree; others a little trite and pedantic. Their students are supposed to meditate upon the prayer, to become familiar with its wording, its rhythm, and its specialized meaning. Then, when they come to use it, it will possess the self-imposed power of exalting them ecstatically to a consciousness of the omnipresence of God who, upon explicit invitation as it were, will be able to act through the individual. The student will come in this way to feel and realize his implicit relationship and necessitous reliance upon God.

For this self-same purpose, the Psalms of the Bible likewise are used by many people. It is needless to indicate that the Psalms breathe a warm atmosphere of adoration, of ecstatic praise of God. Probably the Psalms are the best examples of the beautiful poetry that the Bible contains. The Psalmist knew God at first-hand, had ineffable experience of Him pulsing vibrantly in the heart's blood and in the loins. God, for him, was no metaphysical abstraction to which he wrote these beautiful poems. It was a living presence, strong, vital and passionate. Because of his spiritual experience, the Psalmist had become aware of the supreme reality of this divine intelligence and wisdom and life that abided at the heart of all things. And because he knew this One Life, he adored it and was moved to place his trust completely in it. The metaphysical argument is that by dwelling upon a poem uttered by a spiritually inspired mind, by a mind that knew God in intimate communion, the reader with sympathetic understanding and devotion will find his mind exalted to similar heights of spiritual discernment and realization. Like will speak unto like, and the phenomenon of sympathetic vibration will awaken him to a realization of the divine consciousness within, in a holy and mystical experience.

Psalms most frequently employed for this purpose are the 23rd, 27th, 48th, 66th, 81st, 91st, and the 121st, amongst others. But the first of these seems to have become the favorite. Many commentaries have been written upon it. The 91st psalm likewise is another that has found wide popularity,

Prayer

used the first verse of
e the Chicago conven-
at effect. Other psalms
d seem more than oth-
at majority of students

the use of such poetry
been enunciated with
ient with the idea that
tained a high spiritual
voke a corresponding
ho approach it with all
t to assume that there
words which by itself

works the desired miracle. The words of the psalms are explicit evidence, symbols, of a spiritual state of consciousness. The psalm is the symbol and outcome of a man's spiritual experience. Reading his words, we can be similarly lifted up to the same exalted state of consciousness wherein the Psalmist dwelled.

The prayer does have the effect of stimulating the mind to function in an entirely new way. It creates, if successful, a revolution within the psychological apparatus, a turning around of the mind. It becomes ecstatically uplifted so as to function in a new way, to perceive new and more spiritual ideas, and experience a hitherto never experienced life of divinity and high consciousness. The entire object of prayer, as I see it, is to exalt the mind to an indissoluble unity with God. It must lift the personality on the wings of ardent aspiration in an unrestrained flight of love to a sense of kinship and relationship with the whole of life. And if the prayer does not accomplish this it has failed utterly in its true purpose. Should the individual not respond dynamically and with high fervor, to be raised beyond himself into God, there is a flaw in his employment of the prayer technique.

Chapter Five

Ecstasy

An attitude of cold objectivity and lack of feeling during prayer is, so far as my understanding goes, quite impossible. I cannot conceive how a person who has pondered over the 23rd psalm, for example, and understood it to the extent of employing it as his private and personal metaphysical treatment, can refrain from being strongly moved emotionally. A prayer to be successful should have the effect of bringing about an inner crisis. Eventually it should induce a vigorous emotional reaction that, when understood and controlled and directed, can wing the soul towards the realization of the presence of God, the goal that is ever sought after. A real ecstasy should result, a thoroughgoing standing out of the mind from itself and all its concerns with the body and its problems, from neurosis and inner turmoils. It should raise the individual above his personality, so as to realize his true divine nature. The whole secret of prayer lies in this direction. It aims at ecstatically moving the individual to transcend himself. In short, prayer consists of a complex of psychological gestures designed to enable us to recover our true identity—which is God. In praying, we evolve to the stature of full and perfect adulthood, where we are able to perceive our true and essential relationship to all that lives, and our entire dependence upon the One Mind in whom we do exist and have our being.

Not only is this an intellectual or mental achievement, but the realization itself becomes fired by the rapture that the meditation on prayer should arouse. As a successful operation, prayer must provide scope for man's every faculty. Thus conceived, it is the spiritual and emotional stimulus that is calculated to restore the sense of our original identity with Godhead. Or, at least, it will enable the individual to contact in some novel and dynamic way that boundless source of power and wisdom which we conceive of as God. It is no request to an impossible God for bounty or reward like a child asking presents of its mother or father. Sincerely undertaken, prayer should mobilize all the qualities of the self. Integrity is the essence and goal of its nature. The inner fervor it awakens should reinforce the whole individual, energizing the concept that he holds in mind for treatment so that it becomes realized as concrete reality. This inner fervor is the *sine qua non* of success.

Neville rightly surmises that to make one's prayers fulfill themselves one must go mad temporarily. Even as lovers become excited and moved by the fleeting thought of the sweetheart, so the one employing prayer should react also. He must be capable of becoming so enthused and spiritually excited by the prayer that the whole self lets go of itself and flies direct to its divine goal as though impelled inexorably

Ecstacy

like an arrow from the bow of devotion and aspiration. Success in demonstration comes about not exclusively through human effort, but primarily because the divine force courses through one. First, however, one must have touched adequately the divine universal mind, and right rapture provides the drive towards that goal.

I have always questioned in my mind whether prayer of the quiet unemotional variety is of any ultimate value at all. This cold-blooded petitioning finds no real place within the highest conceptions of spiritual achievement. An ancient mystic and metaphysician once wrote that we should *inflame* ourselves with prayer. And here is the secret revealed in a single word. We must not, counsels Jesus, use vain repetitions as the heathens do. But we may repeat intelligently the prayer again and again until the meaning is driven home, firing us spontaneously to increased devotion.

In his fascinating book *The Psychology of Suggestion*, Dr. Boris Sidis has made an observation which is particularly apropos and pertinent to this discussion. He remarks that "we know that a strange emotion narrows down the field of consciousness." In this way, therefore, suggestions are much more readily accepted by the subconscious mind, than were the mind extensive and preoccupied with a host of sensory perceptions and motor impulses. "We often find," he further remarks, "that people under the emotion of intense excitement lose, so to say, their senses; their mind seems to be paralyzed, or rather, so to say, the one idea that produces the excitement banishes all other ideas, and a state of monoideism, or concentration of the consciousness is thus effected."

Monoideism was the term employed by Braid to describe the hypnotic state, when the subject's attention, all plastic and pliable, could be turned to any one topic, and a total concentration of his mind on that single topic procured. It is for this reason, then, that emotional exaltation is so necessary to metaphysical technique, or to the practice of auto-suggestion, for then the mind's stream becomes automatically narrowed down to a single point, permitting the penetration of the suggestion.

We must so pray that the whole being becomes aflame with a spiritual devotion before which nothing can stand. In that intensity, we rediscover what we always have been in reality. All illusions and errors and limitations fade utterly away before this divine fervor. When the soul literally burns up—"as pants the heart for cooling stream"—then spiritual identity with, or realization of, God becomes more than a possibility. "The desire of Thy house hath burnt me up." Then the heart's desire is accomplished without effort—because actually it is God who prays and God who answers. There is none other to pray, and nothing that can be accomplished save that for which God makes the gesture. The desire that is holy becomes fact—objective phenomenal fact for all to see.

Prayer is a dramatic gesture, implying the utmost in emotional capacity and in spiritual understanding. It bears no relationship to the infantile concept of asking favors of some father-like deity. It is, however, a gesture of realizing the divine reality that has never been obscured, save in the conscious mind. Unconsciously we have always known what we were and to what spiritual power we were related. That knowledge has never been entirely lost. By making gestures of the right and most intelligent kind, we regain a full and conscious realization of our own Godhead.

A study of ancient prayer techniques seems to yield the fact that former authorities, unlike so many today, were not averse to conceiving of prayer as a complex process of autosuggestion. The so-called affirmations of modern metaphysics are quite obviously suggestions. One ancient prayer, or invocation, as once they were called, strongly and frequently employs in its structure the modern usage of "I am" affirmations. For example, it affirms as part of its rubric: "I am He the Bornless Spirit having sight in the feet, strong, and the immortal fire. I am He the Truth. I am He whose mouth ever flameth. I am He that lighteneth and thundereth. I am He from whom is the shower of the Life of Earth. I am He the Grace of the World."

This is the peroration of a long and complicated prayer filled with certain obscure and barbaric elements not altogether comprehensible to the modern mind. There is little doubt however but that the motivating trend of the preliminary parts of the prayer or invocation was gradually to excite the so-called conscious mind of the invoker until a high pitch of fervor was induced. It affirmed the relationship of man to God, narrating the great power and wisdom of God. The intention was that the mind at the critical moment, due to the extraordinary degree of excitement and ardor provoked, should be thrown into a state of high suggestibility. That ardent peak achieved, the peroration containing the potent suggestions was uttered, and the magical results were obtained because the suggestions were accepted and became effectual.

A state of high suggestibility is one during which the normal reticence of the mind to extraneous ideas, the endopsychic resistance of which psychoanalysis speaks, is overcome. This overcoming of the resistance may not necessarily be a permanent conquest. But from the point of view of the prayer technique, that is a matter of very small moment. The resistance is abrogated for a sufficiently long period—a few seconds or a few minutes at most may be its duration—to permit of the immediate acceptance of the suggestions. Once

Ecstacy

in the mind's deeper structure, they can do their work effectively. From within they evoke various states of consciousness that are constantly present though dormant. They are rather like parental imagos present within the unconscious levels of the mind, remaining dormant until mobilized or reinforced by current events or people. The dormancy is overcome by the prayer, and these latent psychic states are stimulated sympathetically into dynamic activity by the suggestions. Suggestions by themselves mean nothing, and of themselves contribute nothing. They only render kinetic previous but unknown contents of the mind.

I am quite willing to admit that to call this process suggestion or auto-suggestion does not in the least render explicable to our minds what we know to occur. A psychological phenomenon of extraordinary interest and power has occurred. We do not know what it really is, but we give it the name of suggestion. Merely to give a scientific term to an unknown process, however, does not necessarily explain it—though this seems to be a common trait of the modern scientific and critical mind. Nor do these terms tell us in what way suggestion works, nor the inner mechanism of its operation within the mind itself. But at least this may be said. The phenomena of suggestion to some extent can be experimentally induced—presuming that we have a good subject and a capable operator—and that goes a very long way for us. This is more than can be said of prayer in its formal religious or even metaphysical sense. I have never heard of any metaphysician who would be willing to "demonstrate" under test conditions. But this is exactly what can be done with suggestion and auto-suggestion. Very severe scientific conditions have been imposed upon experimenters, and these have been satisfactorily fulfilled. And though we do not know in the least the *modus operandi* of suggestion, yet a similar comment can be made upon prayer. We have not the least knowledge how prayer, when successful, operates and how it produces the amazing results which occasionally we do see. For the sake of convenience therefore, we could use the word suggestion and auto-suggestion possibly, in order to convey the same series of ideas as are involved in the idea of prayer.

Moreover, for the sake our own understanding, we can liken the process of successful evocation of inner states of consciousness by means of prayer, which overcomes resistance at the gates of the unconscious levels, by reference to Jungian analysis. The contemplation of dreams in the light of mythological and religio-philosophical processes, awakens out of their latency primordial archetypes that are residues of former cultural periods, to function anew within the conscious sphere. These residues are the psychological imprints, as it were, left by the efforts of former generations of men to solve satisfactorily their own inner and spiritual problems.

As we ourselves become confronted by difficulties of mind and emotion with which we do not know how to deal, the libido, or the mind's energy, under the stimulus of analysis slips away or regresses from the present time into the past. It regresses not merely to infancy, but to older and more ancient levels within the mind where are stored the phylogenetic results of man's age-old attempts adequately to fulfill himself and his spiritual aspirations. These historical records

Ecstacy

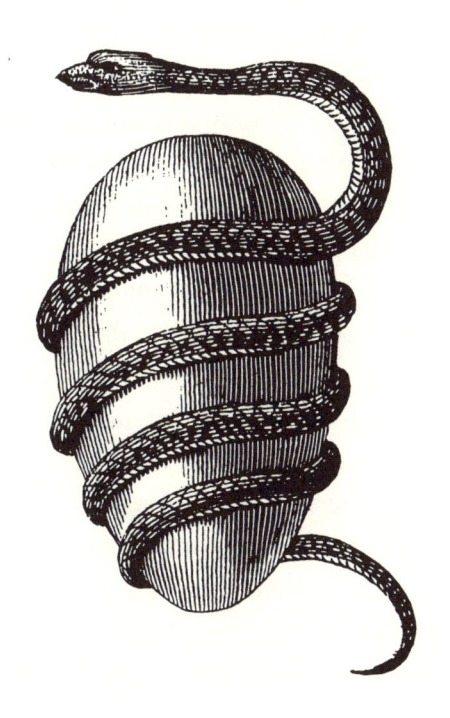

or primordial archetypes of the collective unconscious often assume in dreams the guise of magical processes of old, formerly celebrated religious rites, mythological worship and devotions paid to the old gods. These archetypes, layer by layer, become successively awakened by means of the analytical process. It is as though not merely the superficial aspects of the mind labored to deal with its problems, but every level, every faculty of the whole mind, the whole self, were enlisted in one prodigious effort. In his book *The Integration of the Personality,* Jung devotes a whole chapter to the analysis of numerous dreams of a single person, pointing out how the primordial archetypes were evoked into redemptive activity to bring about this desired process of integration, the achievement of wholeness, of perfection.

Possibly one great advantage of the psalms and ancient prayers or invocations lies in the fact that they awaken memories not merely of infancy but of the far distant past. They bring us in touch once more with the unconscious self hidden deep in our own minds. Therefore, we impinge upon the whole collective background of our individual lives, upon the immeasurable past of duration when the instinctual forces—symbols of powers of miraculous potency and superior wisdom—flourished and prospered and functioned without the conscious interference that belongs to our present day and age. Through such usage of prayer, we recover the vitality and the involuntary higher guidance that obtains in the acquisition of the knowledge of our instincts. Moreover, and what is important for us, we obtain the sense of participating with and belonging to the whole rhythmic stream of life which pulses and vibrates in the world around us.

One of the most outstanding characteristics of primitive man was his possession of the *participation mystique,* an anthropological term to denote that mystical sense of identification with nature, when trees and rivers and clouds, and every phenomenon soever, were alive and spoke to him. Nature was intelligent and peopled widely with dryads and hamadryads, with nymphs, fauns and centaurs. This, today, we would call the projection of unconscious images, the projection as on to an outer mirror of the world of what actually existed within. Primitive man projected his own primitive

Ecstacy

emotions upon all the objects of his world, and not understanding himself within, the things his environment presented to him were similarly primitive and savage and terrifying. It was necessary, as evolution and development proceeded, to break up this *participation mystique,* so that in the rejection of unconscious image-projection the mind would divorce itself from nature and be enormously improved and enriched.

But we have gone too far. The swing of the pendulum has carried us to the opposite extreme. Now we are afraid to see any kind of intelligence in nature outside of our own. We have developed mind to the extent that we have lost sight of the seedling world of unconscious forces within. We have strayed from our roots, and we are lost and stranded with no real sense of direction or guidance. The mind that we evolved has turned out to be, by itself, an empty bubble. Chained to the rock of our own isolation like Prometheus, the vultures gnaw at our vitals. Our own intellectual progress is the very thing that now destroys us.

We are obliged to go forward, to press onwards to the unknown future, not merely to retrace regressively our footsteps to the forgotten past. What we have gained so laboriously in these many centuries of evolution we cannot sacrifice without deliberation, not even for God. And we cannot conceive that God would demand such abrogation of ourselves. That indeed would be disastrous and catastrophic. We would be untrue to our birthright. Instead, we must bring the past up-to-date, as it were. We must recover the former sense of our divine kinship with nature, with things, with men. Then we can press forward, taking with us what we have formerly gained from nature by dint of heroic effort and struggle and experiment.

By adding the past, with its volcanic power and creative force, to the present of reason and logical judgment, a superior combination will have been effected. A true whole will have been engendered. Man will have compelled himself and found the God who abides in the heart of nature. That is a perfection which surely can overcome all problems and difficulties life may present—for the whole man and not merely part of him would be called into active operation. This would truly be evolution, and spiritual development and unfoldment in the finest and highest sense of the term. Metaphysics, if wisely employed, can well become the technique of the future man.

The prayer gesture, therefore, aims to link man by aspiration or by suggestion to the whole vital world of former time when the world was young. That is why prayers and psalms of centuries ago seem to possess so great an efficacy. All harp on the great fundamental truths concerning the power of God in that He created the world, governs it now, and controls all its phenomena. And He can bless His creatures with fruition when they acknowledge Him, as is testified to by so many of the biblical narratives. Thus these prayers tend suggestively to *connect* the individual today, with events and individuals and divine manifestations of time gone by. If God did so much for Abraham and Solomon and Jesus in those days by virtue of their knowledge of Him, then likewise He can do as much today for me if I follow similar rules as did the men of old. A complex process of auto-suggestion is thus set into operation when the requisite degree of exaltation or concentration—the royal effective roads into the Unconscious—have been achieved. And the contemplation of these blessings and wonders evoke similar conditions from within where God abides.

Chapter Six

The Process of Fulfillment

There are at least two attitudes that may be adopted insofar as evolving a satisfactory technique of gestures is concerned. In the one case, the individual ceases to concern himself with whatever it is his problem relates to. He concentrates exclusively on the one idea of God, seeking to let this one idea dominate the whole of his thinking and feeling. In a word, he attempts to let God into his mind. The goal is to become more highly aware of God than ever before, as the one power, the one mind, the one substance of the universe—a presence and power ever potent within. Seeking to become conscious of this divine power within himself, the individual lets it take possession of Him, to identify himself completely with its wisdom and power and substance.

Having done so—or at least made the gesture in that direction—he comes to realize that whatever symptoms of disharmony or lack have prevailed within his environment must disappear. By virtue of his realization of God as harmony and peace and abundance abiding within him, all factors in opposition to this realization fall away. Darkness is no

The Process of Fulfillment

more when the light has arisen. Poverty is meaningless when one has achieved abundance. Conflict within oneself, or with some other member of society, cannot remain unsolved when harmony and peace reign supreme. All problems solve themselves when God is permitted to come in.

The alternative method is principally a modification of the former. It holds similarly that one must let God solve the problems of the individual. As a preliminary, the procedure is as before—to achieve some realization of the one presence and the one power. Sometimes merely recognition is enough. This is a spiritual process or gesture that must take precedence over all others, and can be labelled as the practice of the presence of God. For "unless the Lord build the city, they labor in vain that build it. Unless the Lord keep the city, the watchman waketh but in vain." Having raised the mind momentarily above all temporal considerations, the object of the meditation may be brought within the sphere of the mind. With a well-defined gesture, conscious of the light of God illuminating the mind, and feeling His power throughout every fiber, one passes to the construction of visual images. It is to these imaginative foci that some attention should be given, imagining that the desired result has already been achieved. "Whatever you ask in my name, that I will do."

This latter idea is certainly one of the most outstanding contributions formulated by modern metaphysical movements. Simultaneously it is possibly one of the least understood, from the scientific point of view. Plenty of scriptural authorities are cited to confirm it, but the quotations from the Bible hardly enable us to understand why this method should be adopted. Such treatment of a problem may be satisfactory to some minds, but hardly adequate to the scientific mind that seeks the how and why of things. The rationale of it has certainly not yet been arrived at. None of the explanations is really explanatory. This is proved by the fact that, for example, some of the more prominent metaphysical exponents who are characterized by their sobriety and sanity in writing, hesitate a great deal when recommending this technique. In fact, in his book *Methods and Problems of Spiritual Healing,* Horatio Dresser, who in my estimation is certainly one of the best and soberest writers within the New Thought movement, devotes several pages to a criticism of current metaphysical practice. Most metaphysicians do not hesitate to employ such absolute affirmations as "I am made in the image of God. God is perfect. Therefore, this imperfection, this sickness, this poverty, this problem, is a mere shadow. I deny its existence. It is error, it is false belief. My character is divine, and unspotted. I am perfect, even as God is perfect. I am the temple of the living God." Yet curiously enough, though one finds no vestige of scientific understanding in metaphysical circles, the method is fundamentally sound, based as we shall see upon well-ascertained psychological law.

If a man is out of work and penniless, feeling very inferior and outcast, at night he is most likely to dream that he is a very important person, occupying a major executive position, lording it over hundreds of minions and slaves. A child who is pulled away from the window of a candy store by its

The Process of Fulfillment

impatient mother, may dream that it has a bellyache from eating too much candy. Retire to bed at night slightly hungry and thirsty, and there in the dream will be spread before you a banquet of delectable foods and elegant wines and ambrosia that defy description. Employing the Freudian way of looking at dreams, the deepest needs of the personality dramatically appear in the adventure of the night, not as mere possibilities to be gained some time in the distant future, but as the *fait accompli* now. Scientifically, we have come to regard the dream as a psychic attempt to fulfill needs that would otherwise remain unfulfilled. Every psychologist can forward hundreds of proofs of this contention. In the face of grave problems and insecurity, many will dream of being back in the old parental environment, enjoying the love and security of mother and father. When feeling unloved and neglected, we may even fall back on the forgotten infantile habit of wishing dead someone, a brother or sister or relative, who seemed to receive more love that we did and is therefore responsible for our neglect. An unfulfilled wish means undischarged tension in body and mind. It is because of the high tension created by unconscious and unknown infantile wishes during sleep that the individual seeks to obtain their fulfillment in the dream. His wish is consummated in the dream by unconscious mental processes. This unconscious burgeoning of strong desire relaxes tension to a large extent, so that the person can continue to sleep.

It would be utterly futile, therefore to concentrate during meditation upon the wish to obtain a large sum of money, for example. This desire, until brought to fruition, could only create tension. The deliberate creation of tension when the utmost in relaxation of both body and mind is demanded of the student is to let the left hand not know what the right is doing. Hence, in prayer, to meditate upon need and lack would defeat one's own ends. It would only impress a powerful suggestion upon the unconscious mind, and must create still further need.

He must, in accordance with the unquestionable facts revealed scientifically by dream psychology, imagine himself in possession of that which he craves. The law of his own being must be intelligently and wisely applied. There is thus ample justification for the metaphysical usage of this basic technique. It adopts scientifically the very mechanisms that the unconscious psyche itself employs. The technique resolves itself into an elaborate process of creative fantasy, of dreaming. With this difference, however. He dreams consciously and deliberately. This is no haphazard drifting away from reality into an escape world. It represents a voluntary attempt to touch and alter reality. One can legitimately have faith in the successful working out of what one has asked for, because one employs the laws and mechanisms of nature.

It is not that one turns one's back on the evidence of the senses. To state it in this manner is a complete misapprehension of the problem. The crux of the matter is *fulfillment*—not running away. In fact, the very wording of these metaphysical injunctions reveals the inadvertent attitude, the involuntary motive, of the people who make them. Unconsciously they are escapists. Their language is like the language of dreams—revelatory. They are people who are obliged to run away from

The Process of Fulfillment

certain personal problems here in this world, problems which they feel they cannot or will not solve. Again, unconsciously, they turn away from reality, to wallow, maybe eloquently enough, in a fantasy world, the escape world, which mistakenly they conceive to be the divine order of God. But their metaphysics will not help them ultimately. Aside from their preliminary successes, disaster and frustration loom inevitably ahead. If their secret motive is to escape, they cannot be good teachers, save to similar escapists—however convincing their speech and writing, or fascinating their personality.

We have to remember that we are seeking above all growth, fulfillment. And growth does not imply denial, nor turning away from anything. It means embracing everything, accepting all things. For all that lives is holy, and if we would look deep enough we can find God everywhere. We must work with the weapons forged by our own inner self, to fulfill that self—and that definitely does not mean escape or turning one's back from the evidence of the senses or any other kind of reality.

The metaphysical practice is one of fulfillment through mind, employing the very processes of the unconscious self. The individual takes the process of burgeoning out of the realm of unconscious psychic activity, using it with full and complete awareness of what he is doing. Inasmuch as his mind has become exalted by the previous application of prayer, he has put himself in a highly suggestible state. In this state, the conscious fantasy employs the compensating and burgeoning mechanism of the unconscious psyche, and charges it with affect and strong emotion. Its effect is to thrust the affirmation or picture or fantasy deep within the unconscious levels of the mind. This mind knows no obstacles, recognizes no time, no obstacles which cannot be hurdled. It possesses what Freud calls the "omnipotence of mind," though erroneously he assumes this to be an infantile and therefore false belief.

If the unconscious can be reached in this way, using its own methods, surely miraculous results must follow. It accepts and repeats that which is thrust into it. If we blindly load it down with shame and guilt and fear of impending disaster, what wonder that our environment mirrors forth such things? As Neville has rightly said, the Unconscious or the unconditioned awareness of being is no respecter of persons or of ideas. It will assume the form of whatever is presented to it. "Look upon your desires—all of them," he says, "as the spoken word of God, and every word or desire a promise ... Do not condition your desire. Just accept it as it comes to you ... Such acceptance of your desires is like dropping seed—fertile seed—into prepared soil. For when you can drop the thing desired in consciousness, confident that it shall appear, you have done all that is expected of you." But to accept a desire, means to accept it as already fulfilled.

Therefore no thought of the future or of unfulfillment should be permitted even for one fraction of a second to intrude itself before the attention. "It is finished," cried Jesus. The desire has already, even now, been achieved. Once the fantasy of fulfillment has been created and accepted by the unconscious, it will undergo a process of automatic projection. Unconscious images become projected on to the mirror

The Process of Fulfillment

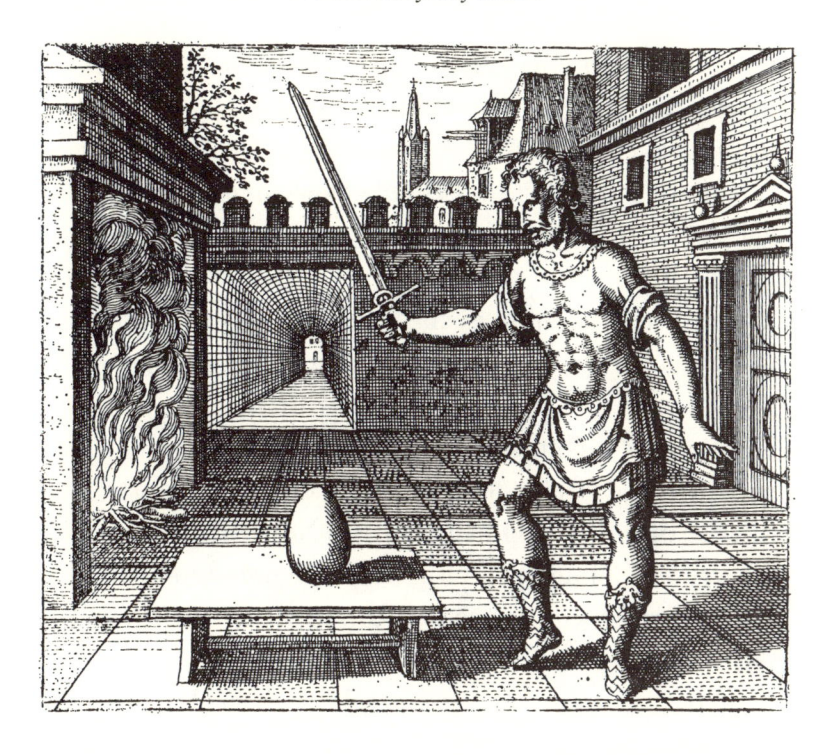

of the external world, and what was once merely a picture or a feeling held within now appears as a reality onto the screen of the world. It is there, complete, before the mind's eye. Not the human eye, for that has been utterly transcended. It is to be seen from God's vision, from the point of view of God, the imminent and transcendent consciousness to whom one thousand years are but as a single day, and who in a twinkling of an eye accomplishes all things. To the Unconscious, the thousandth century before Christ is neither more nor less than the present year. It is a dreamer of age-old dreams, and because of this enormous experience within its being, it is an incomparable prognosticator and magician. What one desires has been envisioned by it from all eternity. What is planned by God, the one universal mind, is that which will be fulfilled. And since it is now in existence, and has been so from the creation of the world, only thanks need to be uttered. Not that God, with whom identification has been achieved, requires a gesture of gratitude. Heartfelt thanks arise spontaneously, coming from a jubilant heart already made gloriously joyful, even gay, by prayerful exaltation brought about through prayer.

And now this thanks uttered, the meditation should be wholly dropped from the mind. The demonstration has come in consciousness. Fulfillment is there. Now the idea needs to be forgotten. Time must be given to the thousand and one details of reality which clamor for our attention. The mind must not be permitted to dwell over long on these interior things once the prayer is done. Into the open fertile field of the mind, the seeds of suggestion have successfully been planted. One can do no more now. The rest must be left to nature or to God. We must be content to leave the matter there, fully confident of demonstration. Nor is this difficult, or asking too much of the individual. Faith is not demanded—that faith which is so impossible for the man who has no faith. Confidence should have been achieved from the relaxation exercises where one discovered that, skeptical attitude notwithstanding, bodily reactions occurred even as the mind was concentrated upon its picture of relaxation. This experience will stand the student in good stead when he finds that he must give up thinking, give up anxiety as to results, for they have been duly achieved in mind. And he knows this and waits—and in the waiting he has achieved success.

This idea has been expressed never more beautifully than in a mystical prose-poem written by an English poet-mystic some thirty or more years ago. I quote the parable as follows:

> The prophet cried against the mountain; come thou hither, that I may speak with thee!
>
> The mountain stirred not. Therefore went the prophet unto the mountain, and spake unto it. But the feet of the prophet were weary, and the mountain heard not his voice.
>
> But I have called unto Thee, and I have journeyed unto Thee, and it availed me not.
>
> I waited patiently, and Thou wast with me from the beginning.
>
> This now I know, O my beloved, and we are stretched at our ease among the vines.
>
> But these thy prophets; they must cry aloud and scourge themselves; they must cross trackless wastes and unfathomed oceans; to await Thee is the end, not the beginning.

It would be indeed a wonderful thing if we could adopt such an attitude. All our strivings are needless. If we would only wait with the spirit of resignation, we would be at the end of our journeys without effort and without useless repining.

Such an attitude would not make for inertia or sterility. On the contrary, we could wait, knowing that the creative work was proceeding satisfactorily within us without effort on our part. We would work and play, not because we must work or that we must relax, but because we would know that this is the way of true self-expression. And in the meanwhile we would wait. The waiting is not merely the beginning of metaphysical demonstration. It is the goal. This is the lesson we must learn.

Chapter Seven

Triumphant Prayers of the Ancients

My task here will be done by reproducing, though without wishing to analyze, some of the prayers or invocations which found favor in former time. Little would be served by dealing more completely with the present practices, prayers and attitudes employed extensively by the metaphysicians today. These can be found in current textbooks. But modern students seem entirely unaware of these ancient prayers and ideas. They do not know that their own efforts have previously been paralleled, sometimes in far more artistic and striking ways. This deficiency I should like in part to remedy.

It is not suggested that these ancient prayers be used today in their entirety. They are not wholly suitable for wide usage. They have no such applicability. But, nevertheless, they do contain ideas and beautiful phrases and profound implications which we would do well to hearken to, and use for our own salvation. If we will be sufficiently open-minded and eager to hear what message they have for us, and not be blinded by mere words which can mislead us, or names which we do not like and therefore deliberately misunderstand, then their significance will shine through. They will come to show profound meaning for all those who read them.

The first of these prayers is based upon an old Egyptian invocation. It was frequently used many years ago by a group of English metaphysicians. The reference to Osiris may put some present-day students off, since they are not altogether willing to read of any spiritual aspiration or prayer that is not solely directed, as it were, to Christ in the manner to which they have been educated. But Osiris, for the Egyptians, was the resurrection of God. He stood as the type and symbol of a man who, having overcome danger and evil in this world through a demonstration of divine power and wisdom, had achieved perfection and redemption, united with the universal life and mind of all things.

> I am Osiris triumphant, even Osiris Onnophris, the justified. I am He who is clothed with the body of flesh, yet in whom is the Spirit of the great Gods. I am the Lord of Life, triumphant over death. He who partaketh with me shall arise with me. I am the manifestor in matter of Those whose abode is the invisible. I am the purified. I stand upon the universe. I am its reconciler with the eternal Gods. I am the perfector of matter, and without me the Universe is *not*.

This prayer combines metaphysical treatment with at least some degree of artistic form, spiritual truth with poetic beauty, and many have found its affirmations of supreme value. The ancient custom was first to imagine the form of the god, a fairly common pictograph, and whilst uttering the prayer to feel that this god-form enveloped the body of the invoker.

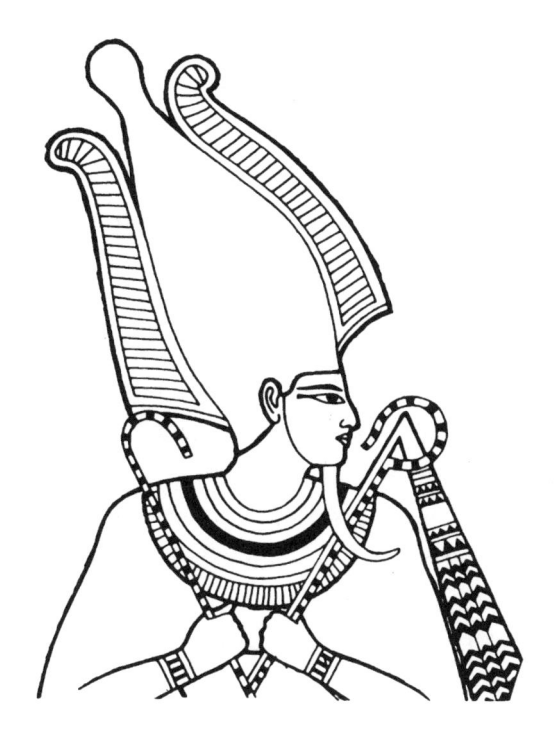

There is another prayer, more or less of the same order in the sense that it employs an Egyptian word or two, which similarly has enjoyed a wide popularity within certain narrow circles. Osiris, as before, can be recognized as implying very much the same series of ideas as Christ, the divine truth that brings freedom and salvation. Amoun the concealed one, represents God as Principle—the universal life and substance that lies behind all phenomena, and to which we are normally blind until and unless we open the eyes of divine mind, the intuition, to realize that though concealed it is yet that One omnipresent power and presence upon which we depend entirely. The prayer is a composite one, combining versicles from several sacred scriptures.

> I am the Resurrection and the Life. Whosoever believeth upon me, though he were dead yet shall he live. And whosoever liveth and believeth upon me shall have eternal life. I am the First and I am the Last. I am He that liveth and was dead, but behold! I am alive for evermore, and hold the keys of hell and of death.
>
> For I know that my redeemer liveth, and he shall stand at the latter day upon the earth. I am the Way, the Truth, and the Life. No man cometh unto the Father but by me. I am the purified. I have passed through the gates of darkness unto Light. I have fought upon earth for good. I have finished my work and entered into the invisible.
>
> I am the Sun in his rising, passed through the hour of cloud and of night. I am Amoun, the concealed one, the opener of the day. I am Osiris Onnophris, the Justified One, Lord of life, triumphant over death. There is no part of me which is not of God.
>
> I am the preparer of the pathway, the Rescuer unto the Light. I am the Reconciler with the Ineffable, the dweller of the Invisible. Let the white brilliance of the divine Spirit descend.

Fairly complex in some respects, this prayer makes its intention clear, dramatic, and simple. Some have regarded it as a thing of supreme beauty, an artistic production of great worth. Study of its clauses will reveal a wealth of idea as to the Christ consciousness, the divine mind, which by prayer and meditation one seeks to re-discover, so that its efficacy may be demonstrated to the world. If approached in the right mood, it possesses the great value of being able to stimulate the requisite degree of rapture and ardor so necessary if desire and need are to be demonstrated in truth.

The next prayer consists of a series of short excerpts taken from a rather long invocation. It is very archaic, has a long history, and is replete with curious philological elements which I doubt would be of much interest to the modern student. The portions that I do quote here have been found by many to be highly satisfactory in preparing their minds for treatment and for spiritual exaltation.

> Thee I invoke the Bornless One. Thee that didst create the earth and the heavens. Thee that didst create the Night and the Day. Thou art Osorronophris (man made perfect) whom no man hath seen at any time ... Thou hast distinguished between the just and the unjust. Thou didst make the female and the male. Thou didst produce the seed and the fruit. Thou didst form men to love one another and to hate one another. Thou didst produce the moist and the dry, and that which nourisheth all created things ... Hear me Thou, for I am the Angel of Paphro Osorronophris. This is Thy true name, handed down to the prophets of Israel ...

Between this preliminary part, a long pause or meditation is supposed to occur during which the student attempts to realize in consciousness the ineffable nature of the Divine Mind, the infinite love and truth and substance that he attempts to know. It is then followed by two sections, as follows:

> This is the Lord of the Gods. This is the Lord of the Universe. This is He whom the winds fear. This is He, who

having made voice by his commandment is Lord of all things, King, Ruler and Helper. Hear me, and make all things subject unto me, so that every spirit of the firmament and of the ether, upon the earth and under the earth, on dry land, and in the water, of whirling air and of rushing fire, and every spell and scourge of God may be made obedient unto me.

The final peroration to succeed this is the prayer briefly noted on a former page as evidence of the ancient's knowledge and employment of the modern affirmation principle.

I am He the Bornless Spirit, having sight in the feet, strong and the immortal Fire. I am He the Truth. I am He who hate that evil should be wrought in the world. I am He that lighteneth and thundereth. I am He, from whom is the shower of the Life of Earth. I am He whose mouth ever flameth. I am He, the begetter and manifester unto the Light. I am He the Grace of the World. The Heart Girt with a serpent is my name.

The reference to hate will possibly prove a thorn in the side of most metaphysicians who prefer to believe that it is only man who creates such so-called "negative" emotions. But it shows that the ancients were a little more willing to face and deal with these highly complex and difficult philosophical problems indicated in the chapters before. If God as the one presence and power is infinite and omnipresent, then there is no room in the universe for aught else beside Him. Man must, therefore, be an integral part of God. If it is man's mind, which in ignorance, and employing his capacity and right of free will, has created what we call evil, even if it is only an illusion and error, then we are still confronted by the fact that the possibility of illusion and error can exist in the divine mind, which is all there possibly can be. I make no pretense towards solving the problem, simply indicating that there is a problem to be solved. And I feel impelled to register the fact that former generations of metaphysicians recognized the problem to exist. We can see the evidences of that awareness in such prayers as that quoted above.

The next prayer to be given here is a lengthy invocation addressed to Thoth. In one sense, the Egyptians were never polytheists. They merely hypostatized various aspects of God. Thoth or Tahuti is the term given by the ancient Egyptians to God, conceived of as wisdom and intelligence and divine mind. Insofar as God is creator, they called him Ptah, the potter, the former of the vast worlds. In His aspect of love, an apparently feminine quality, they addressed Isis, the great mother. His power that manifested as the awe-inspiring phenomena of nature they called Ra Hoor Khuit. His attributes of infinity and omnipresence, they deified as Nu or Nuit, the goddess of infinite space whose body was studded with the gems of the stars. Ra, the Sun, represented light arising in darkness, eradicating the darkness, and illuminating the mind of man with spiritual light. Tmu, the setting sun, and Khephra the midnight sun, are other forms of the Sun god, to indicate that even in the hour of the greatest darkness and sterility of mind, God is always present, awaiting the passage of time before the night passes and ignorance is dispelled.

> I invoke Tahuti, the Lord of Wisdom and of Utterance, the God that cometh forth from the Veil. O Thou majesty of the Godhead, Wisdom-crowned Tahuti, Lord of the Gates of the Universe, Thee do I invoke ...
>
> Behold! I am yesterday, to-day and the brother of the morrow. I am born again and again. Mine is the unseen force wherefrom the Gods are sprung, which giveth life unto the dwellers in the watchtowers of the Universe. I am the charioteer in the East. Lord of the Past and of the Future. I see by my own inward Light, who am Lord of Resurrection that cometh forth from the dusk, and whose birth is from the house of death ...
>
> Behold! He is in me and I in him. Mine is the radiance wherein Ptah floateth over his firmament. I travel upon high! I tread upon the firmament of Nu. I raise a flashing flame with the lightning of mine eye, ever rushing onward in the splendour of the daily glorified Ra, giving my life to the dwellers of Earth.
>
> Therefore, do Thou come forth unto me from Thine abode in the silence, Unutterable Wisdom, all-Light, all-Power ... By whatever name I call Thee, Thou art unnamed and nameless unto eternity. Thou star of the East which didst conduct the Magi, thou art the same, all present in heaven and in hell. Thou that vibratest between the light and the darkness, rising, descending, changing

Healing Energy, Prayer & Relaxation

ever, yet ever the same. The Sun is Thy father, Thy mother the Moon. The Wind hath borne Thee in its bosom, and Earth hath ever nourished the changeless Godhead of Thy youth.

If I say, Come up upon the mountains, the celestial waters shall flow at my word. For I am Ra incarnate, Khephra created in the flesh. I am the eidolon of my father Tmu, Lord of the City of the Sun. The God who commands is in my mouth. The God of Wisdom is in my heart. My tongue is the sanctuary of Truth. And a God sitteth upon my lips. My word is accomplished every day, and the desire of my heart realizes itself like that of Ptah when he createth His works. All things act according to my design, and all things obey my word.

The final prayer which follows is of much more recent composition. It first appeared about a couple of hundred years ago, and has frequently been reprinted. It is a prayer worthy to conclude both this chapter specifically, and the book itself.

From thine hand, O Lord, cometh all good. The characters of Nature with Thy fingers hast Thou traced, but none can read them unless he hath been taught in Thy school. Therefore, even as servants look unto the hands of their masters, and handmaidens unto their mistresses, even so do our eyes look unto Thee, for Thou alone art our help. O Lord our God, who should not extol Thee? Who should not praise Thee?

All is from Thee. All belongeth unto Thee. Either Thy love or Thy anger all must again re-enter. Nothing canst Thou lose, for all must tend unto Thy honor and majesty. Thou art Lord alone, and there is none beside Thee. Thou doest what Thou wilt with Thy mighty arm, and none can escape from Thee. Thou alone helpest in their necessity the humble, the meek-hearted and the poor, who submit themselves unto Thee; and whosoever humbleth himself in dust and ashes before Thee, unto such an one art Thou propitious.

Who should not praise Thee, then, O Lord of the Universe, unto whom there is none like? Whose dwelling is in heaven, and in every virtuous and God-fearing heart. O God, thou Vast One. Thou art in all things. O Nature, Thou Self from Nothing—for what else can I call Thee? In myself I am nothing. In Thee I am Self, and exist in thy Selfhood from eternity. Live Thou in me, and bring me unto that Self which is in Thee.

The Philosophy and Technique of Active Prayer and Surrender

Christopher S. Hyatt, Ph.D.

Rather than being passive, the devotional prayer to which Dr. Regardie refers is active. The reader should think for a moment about the difference. Passive prayer requires a passive belief, a simple hope that the will of the Divine demonstrate itself in the answering of a request. It is based on the master/slave relationship.

Active prayer is both a willful surrendering and a direct full expression of either a specific desire, or more importantly a process of self maturation through surrender and deep expression.

Placing aside the idea of request and answer, we are left with the psychospiritual aspects of "giving over the will" and its total presentation and expression at the same time. This apparently paradoxical statement is in fact an essential process of the building of self-integrity. The integrity or operative efficiency of psycho-bio-spiritual processes is a function of differentiation and co-operation. In essence we are dealing with a multiple tier spiral which is best expressed by body motion, deep emotion and action than by belief systems and linguistic talents.

Remember belief systems have more to do with the desired image one wishes to project and protect than with the depth of psychospiritual knowledge and function. For those who wish to study the difference consult any good book which describes in detail the functioning of the histrionic personality. DSMIII is an excellent reference.

Unlike common or passive prayer, devotional prayer is a living spontaneous occurrence. Its purpose is to kick you out of the expected and ordinary. To cast you adrift in the mystery of life. To bring you out of yourself. Unlike passive prayer which is designed to hold you *in*, active prayer snaps off the shackles of ordinary existence symbolized by belief systems and concepts.

It is not a formalized ritual, although aspects of this may be present, or it can be embodied by formal ritual practice. It is of extreme importance that you are willing to let go of formal images of yourself and prescribed notions of prayer. This time is special, it belongs to you and the GodHead, free of pretense and rigidity, the holding on to dead form.

It is for this reason that active prayer is best done alone or with individuals who are capable of understanding the importance of free expression and surrender.

You do not need to understand *what* is taking place *while* it is taking place. Time enough for that later. What is required is complete trust in the desire to go into yourself as deeply as possible and allow the God(dess) to "enter" you to the depth you are capable of tolerating. In passing, do not assume that you are capable of containing and utilizing the enormous amount of bio-spiritual energy available. Each of us has varying depths and abilities in this area, which can be improved by experience and effort.

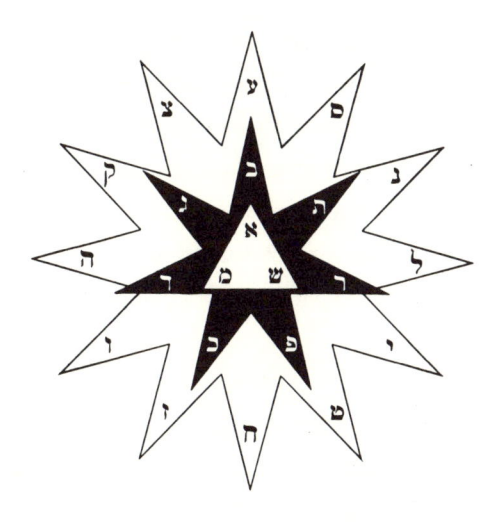

The techniques which follow will help the serious student accomplish this goal.

Prior to devotional prayer, extraneous thoughts and tensions should be transformed. I do not mean gotten rid of, but transformed. This can simply be accomplished through rigorous exercise. A short walk at high speed for example is sufficient to start the process of transformation. Any exercise which increases the depth of breath and brings on a good sweat is ideal.

When this is completed it is wise to rest for 6–8 minutes, feeling the energy pulsating throughout the entire body. Now begin to breathe deeply to a count of 4.

Inhale to the count of 4, exhale to the count of 4. This rhythmic breathing should be continued for at least 5 minutes. When you are finished lie down and sense and feel your body for a moment or two. Now continue the 4 count breath, this time holding the inhale for a count of 8, and then holding the exhale for a count of 8. Do this for 3–5 minutes. Again, sense and feel your body for a minute or two.

Next, curl up into a ball. Be sure that you tense your entire body. You will note that there will be an area or two which might remain relaxed. Do not allow this to occur. Tighten everything up. Hold this position until you begin to feel it "burn." Now hold it for another second more and then let go ... expanding your self to the limits of your imagination. If the situation permits, let out a deep yell or shout.

When you have completed this exercise lie down again and sense and feel your entire body. Begin to become aware of any images which flow through your mind.

Any tension which remains should be dealt with by deliberately tensing the area. Visualize yourself becoming lighter as if you are floating and then begin your active and devotional act of surrender by choosing a prayer or set of words which have a deep significance for you.

You might find some prayer or set of words learned in childhood to have the most "emotional" meaning, even though intellectually you might find them offensive. For the time

Active Prayer and Surrender

being, forego acting on your offensive reaction. Let the emotion build up, as the images and feelings flow through you. Let go into the feeling process. Later you may wish to reform the prayer or set of words into something more acceptable to your present intellectual development.

In fact, a strong offensive feeling is even desirable, since working with it will help you develop and mature your spiritual powers. Remember, do not reject anything. Active surrendering requires complete acceptance. This does not mean, however, that you must approve of what might occur. You can leave this for later, when you begin to integrate your experience with your intellectual belief system. Remember the two are frequently not the same.

As you become more adept at this process you will begin to build a prayer network. This means an integrated and spontaneous set of symbols and feelings which can take you into the depths of spiritual ecstasy at will.

The process of active surrender creates a bond with the Universal Force, which denies nothing and expresses everything. During these experiences you will begin to feel a melting away of the divisions which have separated you from yourself, God(dess), and others. This does not mean that you will feel this way all the time. In fact you shouldn't. Division and Unity are both necessary in the making and manifesting of the Divine presence.

The experience of Unity induced through active surrender softens and intensifies the differentiation process. Therefore you might find that your understanding of events and experiences becomes finer, more whole and complete. Your responses to situations will also become more refined and subtle.

Feelings and events which seemed contradictory or confusing to you will become clearer as less and less of your "model" of the world is imposed on your experience.

Again I feel I must emphasize the difference between sham emotion and feeling and the deep feelings which emerge from devotional prayer. Over the years I have found one good way of telling the difference. Individuals who suffer from sham emotion are very demanding, frequently highly concerned with social image, talk a lot about love and heart, are prone to tantrums and yet are completely unconcerned about anyone including THEMSELVES. To sum it up in two word they make excellent Cheer Leaders.

After completing your devotional session you might find it a good idea to treat yourself to ice cream or some other goody. Savoring the taste of such morsels will reinforce the Sweetness of your experience. However, it is important to remember that while you can enjoy the honey it is not necessary to bring home the bee hive.

The practice of surrender and devotional prayer will help you live your life more fully and openly. As you begin to understand that you have less and less to hold on to and protect you will begin to feel the true freedom of your Divine Will as a living and breathing experience and not as a hope or an idea.

An Alternate Method of Prayer: The Middle Pillar as a Group Working

James Wasserman

Do what thou wilt shall be the whole of the Law.

Dr. Regardie introduced the Middle Pillar ritual to the modern Western Occult Tradition. He stated in *The Complete Golden Dawn System of Magic* that he could find no references to the technique in the original Golden Dawn papers, but was able to trace its origin to Dr. Felkin of the Stella Matutina (a later Golden Dawn offshoot which included Dion Fortune among its members). He says that Dr. Felkin described the ritual in an undeveloped form in one of the Society's grade papers. It was then perfected and popularized by Dr. Regardie in *The Middle Pillar, The Art of True Healing, The Complete Golden Dawn System of Magic* and *The Foundations of Practical Magic*.

I learned the ritual by reading Regardie, as did thousands of others, who were so greatly aided by his writings.

Briefly stated the ritual proceeds as follows:

Healing Energy, Prayer & Relaxation

The first step is conscious relaxation. Do some deep breathing and yoga postures to calm the mind and free the body of deeper stresses and strains.

The Middle Pillar [and all ritual] should begin by attuning the aura and consecrating the psychic space with the Lesser Banishing Ritual of the Pentagram (or a similar rite such as the Star Ruby).

Next, imagine a ball of scintillating white light (say considerably larger than a grapefruit and considerably smaller than a basketball) coalescing both above and interpenetrating with the top of the skull (the Sahasrara chakra or Kether position). Vibrate the Divine Name EHIEH (eh-hee-yeh) several times, while the sphere of Light grows brighter and more vibrant. Regardie suggests at least five minutes.

When the visualization is firmly established, allow the energy to descend slowly through the head and face bathing and rejuvenating oneself, until it comes to the throat. Here the Light coalesces in the Vishuddha chakra or Daath position and is of a pale purple or lavender color. Vibrate the Name YHVH ELOHIM (yeh-ho-vah el-o-heem) until comfortable with the level of concentration, and ready to go on.

Allow the energy to descend through the upper chest region with the same purifying and flowing movement until it comes to the heart or Tiphareth region, being the Anahatta chakra. Vibrate the Name YHVH ELOAH VA DAATH, (yeh-ho-vah el-o-ah vah-daath) while visualizing a sphere of golden light growing richer and brighter.

The Middle Pillar as a Group Working

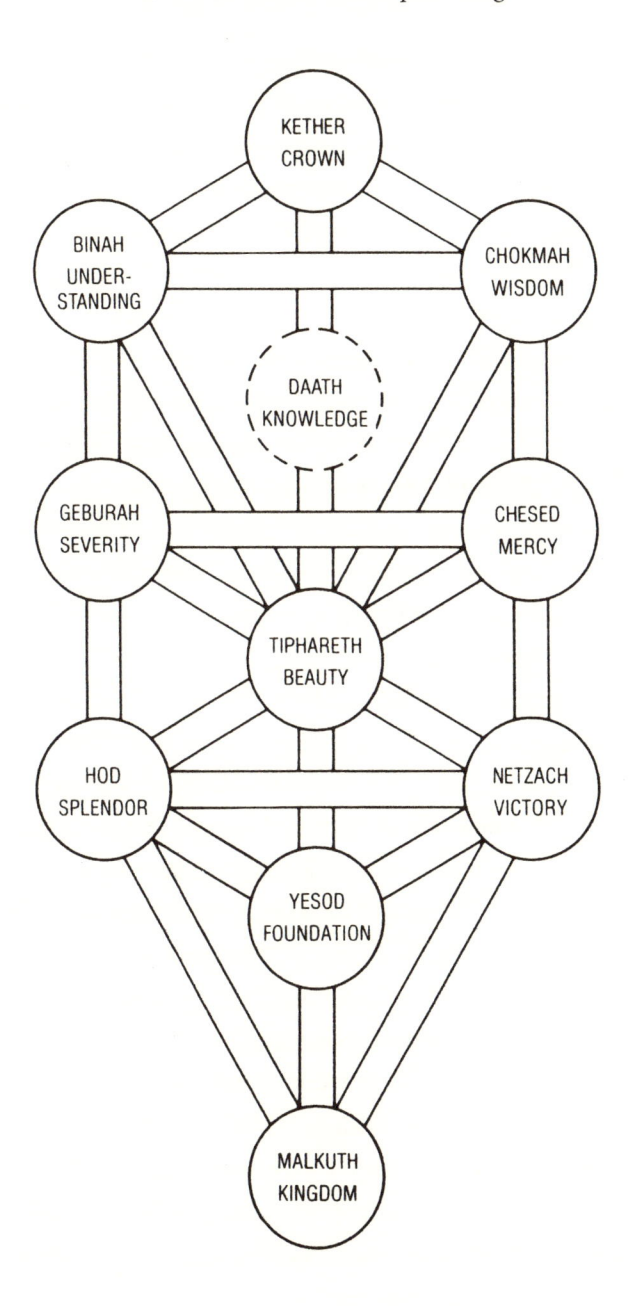

Then take the energy through the solar plexus and stomach, down to the base of the trunk at the genital region, where it meets a sphere of deepest rich purple at the Yesod position or Svadishthana chakra. Here vibrate the Name SHADDAI EL CHAI (sha-dai el chai [there is no equivalent in English to the Hebrew "CH" sound; it is a guttural sound, similar to clearing the throat]).

The energy now descends through the thighs, knees, and shins until it coalesces at the feet in the Malkuth position. Here the crossover to the chakra system is more tenuous although, in my opinion, this position is analogous to the Muladhara chakra. This is particularly evident if one performs the ritual in a seated, cross-legged position. The Malkuth sphere is visualized as deepest vibrating black in color. The Divine Name is ADONAI HA-ARETZ (pronounced as spelled).

Now that the Middle Pillar has been formulated, one visualizes the energy rising through the body, passing upward through the spheres. It ascends from the black sphere at the feet, through the legs to the purple sphere at the genitals, through the stomach and solar plexus to the golden sphere at the heart, through the chest to the lavender sphere at the throat, and up through the face to the white sphere at the crown of the head. Here one concentrates on the glowing white brilliance and begins the work of the three Circulations.

The energy is first visualized as descending down and outward from the crown sphere, along the left side of the body during the out-breath, until it reaches the left foot.

The Middle Pillar as a Group Working

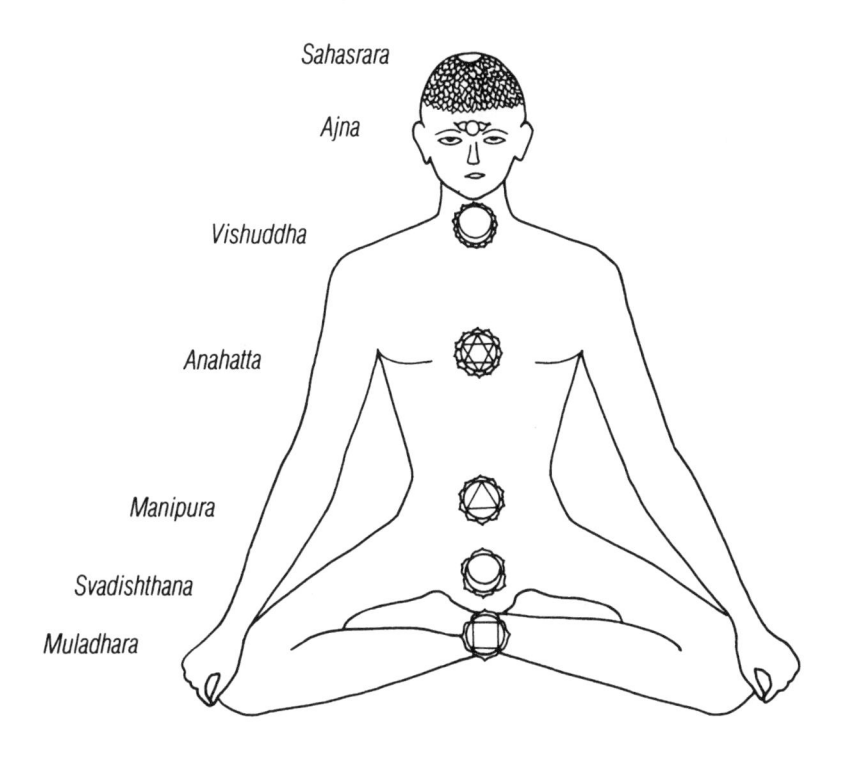

Sahasrara
Ajna
Vishuddha
Anahatta
Manipura
Svadishthana
Muladhara

Then it crosses over to the right foot and ascends, on the in-breath, until it returns to the crown chakra, at the completion of the in-breath. This should be done numerous times until one can feel a flowing motion, timed to the breathing, which is most rejuvenating.

Continue on to the second circulation. It also begins at the crown sphere and goes forward and down the front of the body, on the out-breath, until it reaches the feet. Then, on the in-breath, the energy proceeds up and around the back of the body, until it returns to the sphere of white brilliance at the crown of the head on the completion of the in-breath. Continue to circulate the Light in this manner until it is felt as real (which is easier than it may sound).

Finally, the last circulation is performed. With the energy at the crown, the Light is visualized as descending again through the Middle Pillar, until it reaches the Malkuth sphere at the feet. From here, it is circulated up and through the body to the crown on the in-breath. When it reaches the crown, it is imagined as "fountaining" at the completion of the in-breath, before the out-breath begins. The fountaining energy goes up and out through the crown, and then down and around the body during the out-breath, until it reaches the feet when the out-breath is complete. It is raised again with the in-breath, and the cycle of raising, fountaining and descending continues until the ritual is closed.

Please refer to the image of the auric egg surrounding the body for a more clear sense of the shape of these circulations. Note that the picture is two-dimensional, while the auric egg is not.

Dr. Regardie provides a most interesting discussion of the relationship between the first two circulations and the three-dimensional Tree of Life in *The Complete Golden Dawn System of Magic*. He changed the technique for the third circulation sometime between his publishing of *The Middle Pillar* and *The Art of True Healing*. In the former book, he presented a serpentine spiraling flow for the third circulation. In the latter, he introduced the "fountain" method.

***

The Middle Pillar as a Group Working

When I was first learning the ritual, I was fortunate to be able to discuss it with Dr. Robert Wang, a student and friend of Regardie, and the artist who painted *The Golden Dawn Tarot*. He insisted most dramatically on the importance of practicing the circulations, even in the initial stages of learning the ritual, which Regardie later confirmed to me.

I worked with the ritual for some years, continuing to grow with it and enjoy it. I began to discover the use of the Middle Pillar as a group ritual quite by accident around 1978. I was teaching it to a student and my wife-to-be. The three of us would stand facing one another, and I would recite the instructions to them while we performed the exercise together.

Some years later, while serving as the leader of an occult Lodge, I used the ritual as a guided meditation. There might be up to a dozen or more people working with the visualizations and energy flows, vibrating the Names and doing the circulations in a synchronized manner.

In addition to the basic steps of the ritual outlined above, which were given by Dr. Regardie for individual working, our experience with group working suggested the following considerations.

After the Circle has been banished, there should follow a period of synchronized breathing, and later synchronized mantra, and again synchronized breathing. Until the entire group can breath and chant as one, no attempt should be made to begin the exercise.

The leader should then begin the guided meditation over the sound of the synchronized breathing.

The Middle Pillar as a Group Working

He or she must take the time to carefully prepare the group for any desired activity. For example, the instructions for the first circulation could sound something like this:

> "We will now begin to circulate the energy from the top of the head, on the out-breath, down the left side of the body, to the left foot. Then transfer the energy to the right foot, and raise it, on the in-breath, along the right side of the body, until it returns to the crown. We will begin the circulation on the out-breath. Breathe in … and now out and circulate."

The leader then continues to "talk" the group through the steps until certain that everyone is in unison. The timing is crucial; unless everyone is doing everything exactly together, they are wasting their time.

The leader should stand with the group around the circumference of the Circle. With experience, he or she might, on occasion, risk standing in the center of the Circle (the use of the word "risk" is deliberate as the psychic strain of that geometry is real and should not be attempted until the group is thoroughly coordinated by much practice, and there are no elements in the environment to disrupt the concentration).

Other alternatives began to suggest themselves to us, for example, we adapted Divine Names for the spheres more appropriate to our particular theological aesthetics as Thelemites. These Words of Power were arrived at through a study of *Liber V vel Reguli*, from *Magick in Theory and Practice* by Aleister Crowley.

At the *Kether* point we substitute the Divine Name of NUIT.

At *Daath* we use the Name AIWASS.

At *Tiphareth* we vibrate RA-HOOR-KHUIT.

At *Yesod* we say HADIT.

At *Malkuth* we use the conjoined Divine Name BABALON-THERION.

Working with a group encourages a heightened sense of the metaphysical responsibility of one's magick. For example, during the fountaining circulation, we would raise the energy not only above and through the Circle, but expand it throughout the Universe, bathing all "Planes of Being and By-coming" in the warmth and radiance of the Light.

Further insights came to us which I believe are best left to be discovered by the intuitive process of the group workers, guided by their practice of the ritual and commitment to the Great Work—however, the building of God forms suggests itself as one of the most powerful uses of this exercise.

At the end of the last circulation, we would close something like this: "Now take the energy and focus it at eye level in the center of the Circle. It is in the form of a glowing ball of light that is intensifying in brightness. Hold it in the center of the Circle. It is beginning to shrink even as it grows brighter. It is shrinking, shrinking … and now it disappears into itself … please open the eyes."

There would almost be an audible "pop" when the ball of light collapsed into the Void. The effect of opening our eyes

The Middle Pillar as a Group Working

at once, while being almost painful, was also most effective in maintaining group mind cohesiveness and concentration—and there would be a lightness, an inspired, energized and crisp feeling throughout the Circle.

The Middle Pillar Ritual might be used as the main focus of the evening's work, or as the prelude to other ritual. In either case, it is a most adaptable and energizing exercise, and one we would recommend wholeheartedly to all Western occultists whether for group or individual use.

My thanks to the infamous and magisterial Dr. Hyatt for the opportunity and encouragement (yea, even unto insistence!) to share this experience with the reader, as well as to the members of TAHUTI Lodge for their continued dedication over the years to perfecting this work. And to the friends and loved ones who have helped in the development of this essay. And especially to Dr. Regardie, for sharing the results of his work with all of us.

Love is the law, love under will.

New York City
February 12, 1989 e.v.

The Sacred Ritual of the Pentagram
AIMA

Edited by James Wasserman

[Editor's Note. In 1978, I was honored to meet Reio Nagle at her occult bookstore in Hollywood, CA. We discussed publishing a book composed of eight monographs on occultism written by her late sister under her magical motto AIMA, or Great Mother. I helped Reio by editing, designing, and producing The Ancient Wisdom and Rituals, *published in 1979 by Foibles Publications, and now extremely scarce. This particular essay is the best I have ever read on the geometry of the Pentagram ritual and the Gematria (numerical analysis) of the Hebrew words of which it is formed.]*

Eliphas Levi writes, "The Pentagram, expresses the mind's domination over the elements, and it is by this sign that we bind the demons of the air, the spirits of fire, the spectres of water and the ghosts of earth. It is the Star of the Magi, the burning star of the Gnostic schools, the sign of intellectual

The Sacred Ritual of the Pentagram

omnipotence and autocracy. . . . It is the figure of the human body with the four members and a point representing the head . . . The empire of the will over the Astral Light, which is the physical soul of the four elements, is represented in magic by the Pentagram. . . . Its use, however, is most dangerous to operators who do not completely and perfectly understand it."

The diagram on page 120 shows a pentagram enclosed within a regular pentagon. The actual measurements (allowing for an error imperceptible to the eye, and discoverable only by careful mathematical analysis involving calculations in decimals unknown to our ancient Brethren) are given below. It should be understood that the error (from the standpoint of modern mathematics) is conceded. On the other hand, we have in the literature of occultism many examples of the use of closely approximate whole numbers, used on account of their symbolic sense. A striking example is the use of the number 22 to represent the circumference of a circle whose diameter is 7. The significant numbers represented by the Pentagram are:

1. The number 5, which is the length of the short segment of every Pentagram line.
2. The number 8, the length of the longer segments.
3. The number 21, which is the length of every Pentagram line.
4. The number 105, or total length of the five lines of the Pentagram.

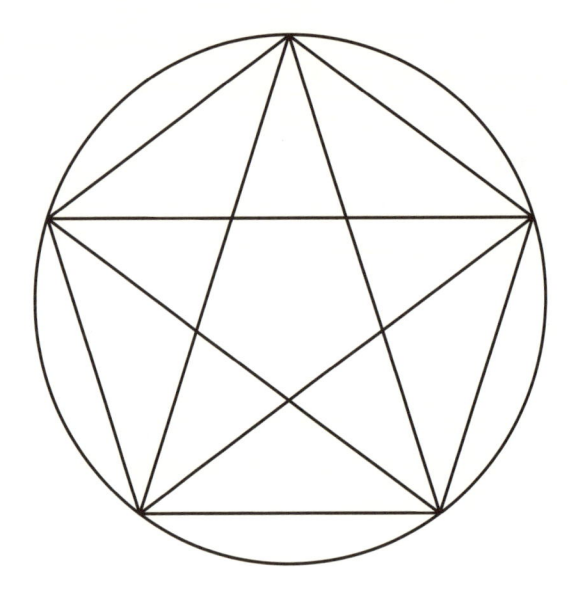

The numbers represented by the enclosing pentagon are:

1. The number 13, the length of a single line of the pentagon.
2. The number 65, the length of the five lines of the pentagon.

The combined length of the lines composing the Pentagram and the enclosing pentagon is 105 + 65 = 170.

Both the pentagon and the Pentagram, as figures corresponding to the number 5, are symbolically related to the planet Mars, to the letter *Heh*, "wherewith creation took place," to the Emperor in Tarot, and thus to the sense of Sight, to the Path of the Constituting Intelligence, and to the zodiacal sign Aries, in which Mars rules and in which the Sun is

The Sacred Ritual of the Pentagram

exalted. Thus the Pentagram is evidently a symbolic resume of the various ideas relating to the following Qabalistic principles.

1. By its connection with the sphere of Mars *(Geburah)* through the number 5, the Pentagram represents the field of the operation of that fiery power whose manifestation throughout the universe strikes terror into primitive minds, whose reaction to its activities is intimated by the name PChD, *Pachad*, "Fear", attributed to the 5th Sephirah. The operation of this same power, to minds advanced enough to perceive the regular and orderly modes of manifestations of this force, do not, as a rule, perceive anything beyond the inexorable exactitude and irresistible might of the Mars-force; so that to them the words "Strength" and "Severity" are the natural descriptions of their estimate of its nature. To some few in every generation, however, comes the higher vision of the operation of this force, and it is the better perception of these seers that is designated by the third and highest name for the 5th Sephirah, DIN, *Deen*, "Justice". Thus to the rudimentary intelligences of the sub-human planes, the Pentagram, as Eliphas Levi intimates, is the sign of FEAR. To men of partial understanding it is the sign of resistless POWER and inexorable LAW. To great seers and sages it is the symbolic affirmation of undeviating JUSTICE.

2. By its connection with the letter *Heh*, the Pentagram is first of all a symbol of creative power; and through the connection of *Heh* in Tetragrammaton with Binah, it is a sign of Intuition and of Understanding. Through the attribution of the letter Heh to the sense of Sight, the Pentagram becomes the magical symbol of true vision, both physical and metaphysical. Through its connection with the sign Aries, it is the magical symbol of those functions of the brain (ruled by Aries) in which the Mars-force is dominant as the energy element, and in which the power symbolized by the Sun has its highest expression (because the sense of sight, both sensory and mental, is really a specialization of light, of which the Sun is the source). All these Qabalistic ideas are related to the 15th Path of the Constituting Intelligence, the mode of Intelligence by which the Universal Mind makes, frames or composes the world-order. The expression of this mode of universal consciousness through a human personal center enables the individual to constitute his own world in accordance with the universal pattern. Thus Eliphas Levi quotes an old magical manuscript to the effect that he who possesses the magical power of the letter *Heh* "can neither be surprised by misfortune nor overwhelmed by disasters, nor conquered by his enemies." The Emperor in Tarot symbolically resumes all these ideas, and properly employed,

The Sacred Ritual of the Pentagram

evokes them from the inner life of the Initiate. Similarly, the Pentagram, as employed in the ritual hereinafter explained, is a symbolic declaration of the same powers.

In tracing a Pentagram, whether on paper or by a suitable magical weapon in the Air, the lines of the enclosing pentagon are not actually drawn, but the points of the Pentagram establish those lines, nevertheless. Hence their meaning shall be our next concern.

Each line is 13 units in length. The number 13 is most important in practical occultism and in Qabalah. Exactly twelve spheres are required to completely enclose a central sphere of the same size. Again, a cube has exactly 13 axes of symmetry, and so has an octahedron. Moses and the 12 tribes, Jesus and the 12 apostles, the Sun and the 12 signs are also references to the inner significance of this number. Furthermore it is the prime factor in the numbers of many important Qabalistic terms. It is the value of the words AChD, *Achad,* Unity and AHBH, *Ahebah,* "Love". Two x 13 is the value of Tetragrammaton, IHVH. Three x 13 is the value of the phrase IHVH AChD, "Tetragrammaton is One". Four x 13 is the value of Tetragrammaton spelt in its plenitude, IVD-HH-VV-HH; of AlMA, "Mother", and of BN, "Son"—all significant words in Qabalah. Five x 13, the number particularly emphasized by the enclosing pentagon is 65, the number of ADNI, *Adonai,* a name which is used in the Pentagram Ritual itself. Thus to trace the Pentagram is to write Adonai geometrically. Sixty-five is also the number of the words HIKL, *Haikal,* "Temple or Palace"; HLL, "to shine, to commend, to praise"; and HS, "be silent". In this connection we may remember the saying: "The Lord is in his Holy Temple, let all the earth keep silence before him."

Coming now to the Pentagram itself, we find that each of its lines is 21 units long. The number 21 is especially important in the Qabalah. It is the value of the three letters IHV with which, according to the *Book of Formation,* God sealed the six directions, or formulated the cosmic Cube of Space. Again, it is the number of the Divine Name, AHIH, *Eheyeh,* which is particularly attributed to the first Sephirah, *Kether.* Thus this number is directly related to the fundamental act of creation, just as the Pentagram is also related symbolically to that act through its correspondence to the number 5. To trace the Pentagram, then, is to make a gesture of identification with the Primal Will; and since AHIH is the God name of *Kether,* also associated with IChIDH, *Yechidah,* "the true Self," the tracing of the Pentagram is a five-fold affirmation of the supremacy and power of that Self.

Why fivefold? Because of the magical and alchemical doctrine that all things are composed of the Quintessence and the four elements. This doctrine is precisely paralleled by the Hindu conception that all things in the universe are composed of *Akasha* and four other *Tattvas* which correspond to fire, water, air and earth. In other words, to trace the Pentagram is to affirm symbolically that the REALITY in all the five modes of cosmic manifestation is none other than the ONE SELF, designated as AHIH, *Eheyeh.*

The Sacred Ritual of the Pentagram

The total length of lines of the Pentagram, if each be reckoned as 21, is 105. This is the sum of the numbers from 1 to 14, or the Mystic Number of 14. Thus, for one familiar with Tarot, to trace the Pentagram is to affirm the full expression of the powers of the ONE SELF portrayed by Temperance. Again, 14 is the number of the Chaldean verb DBCh, "to sacrifice," so that to trace the Pentagram is to make a full and complete symbolic sacrifice of all that stands in the way of free expression of the power of the Primal Will. Fourteen is also the number of the Qabalistic alchemical term ZHB, *Zahab*, (See *Aesch Mezareph*) meaning "gold" and figuratively, "Light." To trace the Pentagram then, is to affirm the extension of that L.V.X. which is the true alchemical gold.

The number 105 itself corresponds by Gematria to three Hebrew verbs. The first is HPK, "to turn, to change, to transform, to overthrow." The second is PKH, "to flow, to run, to pour forth." The third is TzIH, *Tziyah*, "to glow, to burn, to glitter." From this third verb is derived the place-name TzIVN, *Zion*, which has a very important magical significance. Thus to trace the Pentagram is to affirm the operator's power to divert the usual course of force into pre-determined channels, thus transforming magically the appearances surrounding him, and overthrowing adverse conditions (HPK). But all this is accomplished by the realization that the entire world of form is in a state of flux, that the power which assumes the forms of objects in our environment is identical with an *Inner* power, which is none other than the original creative force of the ONE SELF (PKH). And finally, the actual force used in magical operations, the flowing, scintillating, fiery energy which focuses itself in that locality occultly termed TzIVN, *Zion*, is also represented by the total length of the lines of the Pentagram, as representing the verb TzIH, *Tziyah*.

Thus the Pentagram, enclosed in a pentagon, suggests the glowing, flaming (TzIH) manifestation of the Life-power which emanates or pours (PKH) the cosmos, and transforms one expression of itself into another (HPK) in a never-ending series of changes. This manifestation of eternal change is at work within the being of *Adonai* (ADNI = 65 = pentagon), the Lord, whose Self-Existence is the Temple (HIKL = 65) of the Life-power, before whose might the wise keep silence.

The Pentagram, moreover, is directly connected with actual cosmic proportions. Reference has been made to this in speaking of the number 13, but we may go farther. The segments of the Pentagram line (5 and 8) have to do with extreme and mean proportion. Concerning this, Samuel Coleman says the following in *Nature's Harmonic Unity* (a volume written for the instruction of artists, and thus more valuable as a confirmation of the occult positions).

> The series 5, 8, 21, etc., will be seen upon examination to present the nearest integral equivalent to what in the exact science of mathematics is known as "Extreme and Mean Proportion," which may be defined as the *division of any quantity into two such parts or proportions that the measure of the lesser part shall bear the same relation to the measure of the greater part as the measure of the greater part bears in turn to the whole quantity.* In pure mathemat-

ics this interesting proportion produces endless decimals, but Nature knows no fractions and is bound by no decimal divisions, for she produces her harmonies with a free hand and with inimitable perfection, being able to measure her distances and proportions with the extremest mathematical nicety yet without being subjected to the need of the cumbersome calculation which man would be obliged to use in her place. Nature's protractor is always right, and in her use of infinite subdivisions the smallest humanly conceivable fraction would seem to her a whole number. For ready service, therefore, this continuing series of 5, 8, 13, 21, 34, 55, etc., will be found to be one of immense use where absolute exactness is not requisite, since by the employment of these whole numbers the enormous effort required by the employment of fractions involved in precise extreme and mean proportion is escaped. If we bear in mind, that the ancient systems of mathematical numeration were incapable of handling fractions with our modern facility, we shall understand more clearly why the Egyptians and Greeks did not treat fractions as "numbers" and why they so habitually substituted an integral approximate in place of our decimal precision.

For practical purposes then, we may say that whenever we draw a Pentagram, we also divide each of its five lines in extreme and mean proportion. That is to say, we make the measure of the lesser part bear the same relation to the measure of the greater part as the greater part bears to the whole line. The symbolic meaning is obvious. In using the

Pentagram we always apply the measure of the lesser part, which represents the particular problem, to our human powers and possibilities, which correspond to the greater part. We also indicate that our powers are related to that problem in exactly the same way that we ourselves are related to the whole line, which represents the word AHIH, *Eheyeh*, that is to say the Self-Existence of the Primal Will. In other words, the formulation of the Pentagram is a symbolic assertion that law pervades all manifestation, that we are ourselves in the same relation of control with respect to that which is below us as is the Self-Existence of the Primal Will in relation to us.

In other words, by making the Pentagram ceremonially, we symbolically recognize that we are absolutely under the direction of the Primal Will, and that this direction is manifested through the operation of unchanging law. At the same time we symbolically affirm the fact that we have over our problems and circumstances the same power of control which the One Existence has over us—a power likewise expressed through unchanging law.[1]

This is the essence of the significance of the Pentagram. Its ceremonial use in the Invoking and Banishing Ritual is explained as follows:

---

[1] The Pentagram lines are subdivided in EXACT extreme and mean ratio, geometrically. It is only the numbers 5, 8, and 13, that are symbolic integral approximations. That is to say, the 13 unit segment. Also, the 8 unit segment is to the 5 unit segment as is the 13 unit segment to the 8 unit segment. These ratios are rigorously exact and subject to geometrical proof. (AIMA)

The Sacred Ritual of the Pentagram

The Ritual of the Pentagram corresponds in every detail to the mathematical and Qabalistic meaning of the figure. It may be performed with either a dagger or sword. Any pointed instrument of steel will do but it should not be used for other purposes. Before using it for the ritual, pass the blade through the flame of a candle and wipe it off with a piece of silk. If kept solely for the purpose of the ritual, it will not be necessary to cleanse it with fire again. Steel is used because it is the metal corresponding to Mars, and because it has certain occult affinities for certain of nature's finer forces. Make for it a bag of red silk and keep it wrapped in this when not in use. This insures it being associated in fact, and in your consciousness with the Mars vibration.

At the beginning of the ritual, the operator faces East, that is, toward the place of dawn, and toward the place of *Kether* on the Tree of Life. By so doing he symbolically affirms the truth that all his power is derived from the One Source of Light and Life which is manifested to us as the Sun. In performing the operation, he is technically in the position represented on the Tree by the point at which the Paths of *Samekh* (Sagittarius) and *Peh* (Mars) cross each other, between *Yesod* and *Tiphareth*. If you have a Sanctum, it would be best to place your Altar so that you can walk around it. If you have neither Altar nor Sanctum, any quiet place where you will not be disturbed will do. Stand midway between the Altar and the East wall of your room and face East. (Or, stand facing East wherever you are about to perform the operation.)

The first step of the operation is the formulation of the Qabalistic Cross. While this is being made, the magical sword or dagger is held point upward in the operator's left hand, leaving the right hand free for the following action:

1. Touching your forehead with the forefinger of your right hand, intone or say: *Ateh.*

This name, which is AThH equals 406, and means "To Thee," or simply "Thou." This name is numerically equivalent to the letter-name *Tau*, (ThV.) This number is important because it is the second "Theosophical extension" or Mystic Number from 7. That is, the sum of the numbers from 0 to 7 equals 28, and the sum of the numbers from 0 to 28 equals 406. The number 406 represents the following words in Hebrew: OMHARTz, *Aam ha Eretz*, "an ignoramus", literally "man of earth, a clod"; VPSRIN (Dan. 5:25), pronounced *Upharsin*, means "divided"; SHVQ, *Shoke*, "to join closely, to run," also "the leg (of man or beast)"; and ShNVIM, *Shanaim*, "repetitions, changes, transformations." Thus the first word of the ritual has to do with the transformation of the "man of earth" into a conscious vehicle of the Creative Power, through conscious union of personality with the Administrative Intelligence associated with the letter *Tau,* and symbolized by Key 21 of Tarot.

2. Touching your breast, intone: *Malkuth.*

Malkuth (MLKUTh) signifies "The Kingdom" and is primarily a recognition that whatever occurs is part of the Cosmic Order. A perfect order too, since the number of MLKVTh is the "perfect number" 496, the sum of the numbers from 0 to 31 and thus by implication the complete extension of the powers represented by the divine name AL, EL (equals 31), which is attributed to *Chesed*.

(Note that the number of *Malkuth* on the Tree is 10. The Mystic Number or Theosophical extension of 4, which is the number of *Chesed*.) Furthermore, 496 is the value of VTh-MIM, *Ve-Thummim*, "and perfections." The whole significance of this second step in the ritual is the affirmation of the Cosmic Order proceeding from the divine self-impartation represented by *Chesed* and 4.

> 3. Touching your right shoulder, intone: *Vey-Geburah* (VGBVRH) 222.

Thus the third step of the ritual is directly related to the 5h Sephirah, *Geburah*, Severity, Strength or Justice.

> 4. Touching your left shoulder, intone: *Vey-Gedulah* (VGDVLH) 54.

54 is the number of DN, *Dan* "judgment," the name of the Hebrew tribe corresponding to Scorpio, the night house, or occult sign ruled by Mars. This step corresponds to the 4th Sephirah, in the aspect of Magnificence, or *Gedulah*.

> 5. Clasping your hands upon your breast, but keeping the fingers open, so that the fingers and thumb make five crosses, and represent the 10 Sephiroth

Healing Energy, Prayer & Relaxation

(with the magical weapon held by the hilt between the palms, point upward) intone: *Le-Olahm,* (LOVLM) 176.

This means "Throughout the ages."

You then conclude this affirmation of eternal dominion, power and glory to the ONE SELF by pronouncing or intoning the confirmatory word: *Amen,* (AMN) 91, or 7 X 13.[2]

Phonetically, the complete sentence composed of the six Hebrew words is: *Ateh, Malkuth, Vay-Geburah, Vay-Gedulah, Leh-Oh-Lahm, Ah-men.* The words should be said in a resonant, vibrating voice.

There are five steps in this part of the ritual. The total enumeration of the words employed is also a multiple of 5. (AThH, 406 + MLKVTh, 496 + VGBVRH, 222 + VGDVLH, 54 + LOVLM, 176 + AMN, 91 equals 1445). 1445 is the number of the phrase LShAIRITh NChLThV, "the remnant of his heritage," which, of course, has direct application to any human use of the Life-power's energy. 1445 is also 5 x 289, and 289 corresponds to PTR, "to break through, to liberate," and to PRT, "to distinguish, to particularize." Both verbs designate the kind of activity represented by the Pentagram, as well as the actual purpose of the Pentagram Ritual

---

[2] Compare the above with the concluding words of the "Lord's Prayer", "Thine (Attah) is the Kingdom (Malkuth) and the power (Ve-Geburah) and the Glory (Ve-Gedulah) forever and ever (Leh-Olahm,) Amen." (AIMA)

The Sacred Ritual of the Pentagram

which aims to bring about a particular manifestation of the Life-power's liberating energy, and comprehends that energy as working in a five-fold manner. Observe too, that the letters which form these verbs are the same, differently arranged. Each begins with *Peh*, the letter of Mars. Each includes *Resh*, the alphabetical sign of the Sun. In both we find *Teth*, symbol of the serpent force and of Leo, the zodiacal sign corresponding to the Sun.

Now, still facing East, draw a Pentagram in the air before you, tracing it with the point of your magical weapon, held in the right hand.

Great care must be taken to close the Pentagram at its starting point.

The Invoking Pentagram begins with a downward stroke and the lines are traced in the direction as shown. The Banishing Pentagram begins with an upward stroke. Each Pentagram is traced as a continuous line. (See diagrams on the following page.) Trace the figure in the air before you, just as you would draw it on the wall. Let the arm be fully extended during this part of the operation, and trace each line with a measured deliberate sweep of the arm. Practice this part of the operation until you can make the figure firmly and exactly without any trace of hurry or hesitation.

After the tracing of the Pentagram, extend your right arm, holding your weapon so that the point is directed toward the center of the Pentagram. Then take a deep breath and while exhaling pronounce or intone the Divine Name, IHVH. Only the letters are pronounced ... *Yod Heh Vau Heh*.

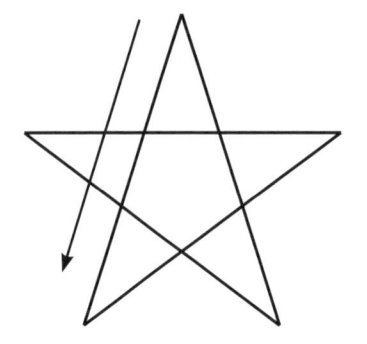

The Invoking Pentagram is begun at the top, and the lines are made in the directions shown by the arrow. Note that the movement used in making the lines is similar to that of a spiral drawn counterclockwise.

The Banishing Pentagram is the reverse of the Invoking. It is begun at the lower left hand corner, and the lines are made in the directions shown by the arrow. This movement is like that used in describing a spiral drawn clockwise.

At the same time you should endeavor to visualize the Pentagram as a flaming star of electric fire, bluish white.

You then turn to the South, continuing to hold your arm extended, as if tracing a line from the center of the Pentagram at the East to the point which will be the center of the Pentagram traced at the South. As you do so, try to see mentally, a line of the same electric fire traced by the point of the weapon. Facing South you make another Pentagram and again, advance the point of the weapon toward the center of the Pentagram. This time you say or intone the Divine Name: *Adonai*, ADNI.

You then visualize the Pentagram as before.

The Sacred Ritual of the Pentagram

Now turn or move to the West, holding the weapon extended as before, and repeating the mental vision of the line of electric fire. At the West the same tracing of the Pentagram is repeated, but the Divine Name said or intoned is: *Eheyeh,* AHIH.

You now move to the North and make a fourth Pentagram.

Here say or intone the *Notaricon*[3] AGLA. Many writers ignore the fact that this "word" is actually composed of the initials of the sentence: *Ateh Gebur Leh-Olahm Adonai,* AThH GBVR LOVLM ADNI. This signifies "Thine is the power throughout ages, O Lord!" The total numeration of the words in this sentence is 858, in which the succession of digits is a numerical representation of the proportions of the three segments of a Pentagram line. 858, moreover is 66 x 13, and 66 is the Mystical Number of 11, a number which is especially connected with the Magic of LVX because it is that of AVD, *Od,* the force used in beneficent magic.

From the North, you now return to the East, tracing the line as before, until it reaches the central point of the first Pentagram, and thus completes the circle of electric fire.

Face East, extend your arms at full length on either side, so that your body and arms form a cross, holding the weapon point upward in your right hand. Here you intone the following Angelic Names:

---

3 [A Qabalistic word formed from the initial letters of a sentence.—Ed.]

1. Before me, *Raphael* (RPAL: 311)
   Visualize the archangel as a mighty figure in a yellow robe in which shimmers the complementary mauve. As the East is the station of Air, you may mentally feel a gentle breeze coming from around the figure.

2. Behind me *Gabriel* (GBRIAL: 246)
   Visualize this archangel behind you robed in blue with orange complementary tones, and a crystal cup of blue water held aloft in the hands. The West is the station of Water, so you may sense water flowing from behind the figure.

3. At my right hand Michael (MIKAL: 101)
   Visualize the glowing archangel at the right as dressed in robes of red, with vivid green overtones. A great sword of steel is uplifted in the hand. The South is the station of Fire, so you may sense radiant heat and flames.

4. At my left hand Uriel (AVRIAL: 248)
   Visualize the archangel at your left as robed in a parti-coloured robe composed of citrine, olive, russet and black. The North is the station of Earth so you may visualize the figure on a fertile ground with grasses and wheat .

5. Around me flame the Pentagrams, above me shines the six-rayed star.

The Sacred Ritual of the Pentagram

You then repeat the formula of the Qabalistic Cross. This completes the Pentagram Ritual.

The purpose of the Invoking Ritual is to put you in contact with the higher forces. It makes the personal organism a center of expression for a strong current of the Astral Light. It should be used sparingly, preferably in the morning. It may also be employed just before beginning some undertaking which makes a great demand upon the strength of the Operator.

The purpose of the Banishing Ritual is protective. It may be used more often than the Invoking Ritual, for its object is to raise the personal vibrations to a point where they repel all adverse influences. In ceremonials involving the employment of the "inhabitants of the elements" as they are called in the *Fama Fraternitatis,* the Banishing Pentagram serves to avert any danger of obsession. In using the Pentagram Ritual you are dealing with no other inhabitants than the gnomes or spirits of earth. When you are thoroughly perfected in the actual performance of the Pentagram Ritual, you may perform it mentally. Simply imagine every step of the process and be careful to throw the whole weight of your magical will into every stage of the physical operation.

The Divine Names used in this ritual are expressed by the proportions of the Pentagram. For the first of these, IHVH, it is necessary to take a different unit-measurement of the lines of the figure. If we take a single line as having a longer segment of 8 and a shorter segment of 5, then the longer segment is to the shorter as 1.6 is to 1, for

$$8 : 5 : 1.6 : 1$$

Healing Energy, Prayer & Relaxation

Using this proportion, the unit length of a single line will be 4.2. Then the five lines will have a total length of 21, and they will be enclosed by a regular pentagon, each of whose sides is 1 unit long. Adding the length of the lines and the length of the sides of the pentagon, we get 21 + 5 which equals 26, the value of IHVH, Tetragrammaton. The same result will be gained by adding the perimeters of the five isoceles triangles forming the points of the star to the perimeter of the enclosed pentagon.

The Divine Name *Adonai,* ADNI, is represented by the five longer segments of each line of the figure, when the unit measurement, of a single line is taken as 21. It is also represented by the regular pentagon enclosing the Pentagram, for although this is not traced, its position and proportions are established by the points of the figure. For ADNI equals 65 equals 5 x 13.

The Divine Name *Eheyeh,* AHIH, equals 21. This is the total length of the Pentagram lines, if each be taken as 4.2. It is also the sum of the perimeters of the five isoceles triangles forming the points of the star, using the same measurement. Again, it is the length of each Pentagram line when the measurement of the longer portion is 8, and of the shorter 5.

The sentence, ATh GBVR LOVLM ADNI, *Ateh Gebur-Leh-Olahm Adonai,* (AGLA) as mentioned adds to 858, so that the sequence of the digits represent the integral expression of the unit-values of the three parts of the Pentagram line.

Tetragrammaton, IHVH, is pronounced at the East, because it designates the Self-Existent ONE. The East is the point of the compass symbolizing beginning or dawn, and the beginning of all magical works is the fact of Self-Existence. This name definitely ascribes the powers invoked by the operation to their true source.

Eheyeh, AHIH, the Divine Name attributed to *Kether*, is pronounced at the West because the West is the place of sunset, and so represents the completion or end of the Sun's daily journey. The West is thus the symbol of completion or end goal of all human endeavor. The name AHIH is associated with it in order to remind us that the object of all magical works is the operator's identification with the Primal Will, or *Kether*. *Kether* is also the seat of *Yechidah*, IChIDH, the true Self, and all magic has for its object the actual expression of the latent powers of *Yechidah*. Ours is a work whose End is its Beginning, even as the ancient picture of the serpent with its tail in its mouth is intended to remind us.

Adonai, ADNI, "Lord," is the Divine Name particularly attributed to *Malkuth*, the Kingdom. It represents what Hindus call *Ishvara*, or the Self-Existent ONE as the ruler of the Kingdom of the personal LORD. This name is pronounced in the South, the place of the Sun's meridian height, as a reminder that our immediate connection with the Self-Existent ONE is through the agency of ITS manifestation as the solar radiance.

The *Notaricon* AGLA representing the sentence, *Ateh, Gebur Leh-Olahm Adonai* (ATh GBVR LOVLM ADNI), "Thine is the Power throughout the ages, O Lord," is recited at the North because the North, as the place of the greatest symbolic cold and darkness, represents the latent or unmanifested (cold) forces of the universe, and our ignorance (darkness) as to their real nature. The North is the place of the Unknown, the region of appearances and errors. Therefore it is the direction associated with the letter *Peh,* and with the 16th Key of Tarot, which shows the overthrow of the structure of false knowledge by the lightning-flash, which typifies the Tree of Life, or knowledge of Reality. Hence, in the North is said the sentence which sums up the whole esoteric doctrine, ascribing ALL power, unknown and unmanifested, as well as known and expressed, at ALL times, to the One Source of all. This sentence is the mathematical formula 858, which shows the Rhythm of the Cosmic Breath (8), working through the mathematical order of the universe (5), and continually reproducing the process whereby the Life-power involves itself in the limitations of form, and evolves itself again from the bondage of those limitations (8).

When the operator returns to the East, he stands with his arms extended, so as to form a cross. Thus he identifies himself with the Administrative Intelligence, represented by the letter *Tau* and by Key 21 of Tarot. In so doing he symbolically affirms the Divine Mercy and the Divine Justice, because a man standing erect with arms extended so as to form a cross, defines the boundaries of an imaginary square. This, because in normally proportioned human bodies, the distance from fingertip to fingertip, when the arms are extended, is equal to the height of the body. Hence this position represents the same basic idea as that suggested by the Square, and by the number 4. Furthermore, it affirms the complete manifestation of the 10 Sephiroth in the 4 worlds, since the Qabalistic

The Sacred Ritual of the Pentagram

idea is that each Sephirah includes the powers of all 10 Sephiroth. Thus the number 400, which is the value of the letter Tau, is the number of total manifestation.

The operator then recites the names of the Angels of the four points of the compass. He says, "Before me, Raphael," because he faces East. In this position, the West is behind him, and as its Angel is Gabriel, at this point the ritual runs: "Behind me, Gabriel." The South is at his right hand, and its ruler Michael, is designated by the sentence, "At my right hand, Michael." Uriel, or Auriel, ruler of the North, is referred to by the words, "At my left hand, Auriel."

Raphael, RPAL, means "God is the healer." The name is derived from the verb RPA, 'to bind up, to save, to restore, to support". It refers to the East, as does the divine name IHVH, because the beginning of all magical works is the recognition that the Self-Existent One is the only support of human undertakings, the only power that can coordinate (bind up) and make whole or complete any of the works of man.

Gabriel, GBRIAL, means "Strong one of God," and comes from the same root as *Geburah*. It is referred to the West, because the completion of all magical works is due, not to the operator's personal power, but to the fact that the operation makes him an open channel or transparent medium through which the Life-power's activity of adaptation (corresponding to the power of the 5th Sephirah) may be freely expressed.

Michael, MIKAL, "Like unto God," is referred to the South as is *Adonai*, ADNI, because this Name is intended to remind the operator of the identity of his personal "Lord" with the Supreme Spirit.

Uriel, AVRIAL, "The enlightened of God," is referred to the North, and associated with the *Notaricon* AGLA intoned at that point, because enlightenment consists in the knowledge that ALL powers, no matter how they appear, are rooted in the Divine Self-activity.

The four Angels invoked in this ritual have also other Qabalistic meanings. Raphael is the Angel of Mercury, and of the element of Air, and is for this reason attributed to *Ruach* in the Qabalistic classification of the parts of the human constitution. Gabriel, Angel of the Moon, corresponds to the element of Water, and to *Neshamah*, the Intuition. Michael, Angel of the Sun, corresponds to Fire, and *Chiah*, the Lifeforce. Uriel, Angel of Earth, corresponds to *Nephesh*, the Animal Soul, or body consciousness.

The sentence, "Around me flames the Pentagram" refers to the intellectual perception that since the Pentagram is mathematically the symbol of Divinity, as heretofore shown, and also the symbol of Man, the microcosm, it follows that the operator is looking forward to a realization of the real identity between the Self in human personality and the Self-Existence designated by IHVH. Full consciousness of that identity is the completion of the Great Work. It is the making of the mystical "Stone," the ABN, *Ehben*," in which AB, Father and BN, Son are perfectly conjoined.

The sentence, "Above me shines the six-rayed Star" refers to the Hexagram, the Star of the Macrocosm, or Great Universe. The Hexagram is composed of six equilateral triangles formed by the intersection of two great equilateral triangles representing Fire and Water. Each of the six lines composing

The Sacred Ritual of the Pentagram

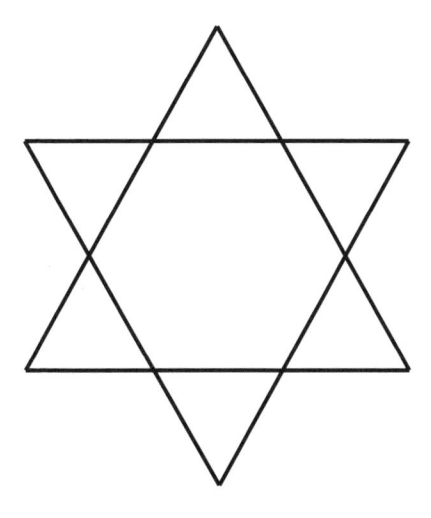

the Hexagram is divided into exactly three equal parts, so that the total length of the lines is 6 x 3 = 18, the number of the word ChI, *Chai*, "Life". The sentence in the ritual therefore means, "Above me is the entire force of the Cosmic Life."

Since a single line of the Hexagram contains three equal parts, each of which may be represented by the number 1, every line may also be symbolized by the number 111. This is the number of the letter-name ALP, *Aleph*; of the adjective PLA, *Pehleh*, "Admirable of Hidden," which designates the first Path on the Tree of Life, *Kether*; of the initials of Brother P.A.L. who was the associate of Brother C.R., Founder of Rosicrucianism, at the beginning of his journey to the Holy Land; of AOM, the Hebrew equivalent of the Sanskrit AUM; of APL, *Ophel*, "darkness, obscurity," (the obscurity of the No-Thing which precedes manifestation); and of OVLH, *Olah*, which has three meanings: 1) "Wickedness, Injustice," and refers to the apparent iniquity of some phases of the cosmic manifestation; 2) "a step, a staircase," which refers to the graded ascent of evolutionary development, 3) "a burnt offering, a sacrifice," which refers to the self-offering of the Life-power in the perpetual sacrifice of the cosmic manifestation.

Since a single line of a Hexagram may be represented by the number 111, the six lines represent 6 x 111, or 666. This is the number which has always had a definite connection with the Sun, and here it may be noted that on the Tree of Life the number 6, of which a Hexagram is the geometrical symbol, is the Sphere of the Sun. Furthermore, the magic square of the Sun contains the numbers from 1 to 36, so that the total resulting from adding all the numbers in such a square is 666, the Theosophical extension, or Mystic Number of 36.

666 is the number of the names SVRTh, *Sorath*, "Spirit of the Sun"; of SHMSh IHVH, "Tetragrammaton of the Sun", or "Sun of Eternity"; and of NRVNOSR, the Hebrew spelling of Nero Caesar. 666 is also the celebrated number of the Beast mentioned in Revelation.

When the human mind accepts the life processes of the macrocosm, symbolized by the Hexagram, as final determinants of human action, it accepts fatalism. Then it is, as Jacob Boehme would say, "under the domination of the astral spirit." For the hexagram is the figure which is used to divide a circle into twelve equal parts, representing the Signs of the Zodiac and the Houses of Heaven used in Astrology. To think of human beings as absolutely dominated by the forces of the macrocosm is to accept materialism, and when thorough-going materialism is carried into practice, it leads to bestial conduct.

The Sacred Ritual of the Pentagram

Many observers of history have perceived that materialism is the characteristic mental attitude of what may be called the "Roman" interpretation of life. It is the point of view which makes a god of blind force. Politically, it is expressed in those attitudes which justify war as a biological necessity, and make brute strength the only test of the "survival of the fittest."

Many people feel that this idea, which permeates the traditional political philosophies of many European nations, and vitiates their systems of jurisprudence, may be traced directly to the Rome of the Caesars. It is undoubtedly older than Rome, but in the Rome of the Caesars, it dominated the world for a time.

If we realize this, we shall find ourselves in agreement with those interpreters of the *Book of Revelation* (the sanest and least fanatical of all who have tried their ingenuity on the riddle of that dark book) who believe the number of the Beast to be a reference to Nero, from the Hebrew NRVNQSR. Nero personified the materialistic conception of human life. This conception continues to poison the life of the world to this very day.

Its root is the belief that the physical forces are the only real forces, that the laws of the physical are the only real laws. From this root springs the false doctrine of determinism, false because it does not follow the idea to its logical conclusion, which makes of men, puppets moved by the strings of blind force and necessity.

Opposed to this doctrine is the magical conception summarized in the Ritual of the Pentagram. This says that man, with the powers of nature and of evolution (symbolized by the Hexagram) behind him, may so utilize and direct those forces through the agency of human personality as to produce, by artistic adaptations, results which go far beyond the macrocosmic averages. The Pentagram which is a symbol of the Logos made flesh, which announces the identity of the Self-existent ONE with the essential Self in man, is an emblem of this work of adaptation.

Man himself is the subject of his own alchemical operations. By artistic adaptations of macrocosmic powers focussed in his personality, man may modify himself, even as he has succeeded in modifying the animal life in his environment. He may tame the wild animals in his own cell-structure. He may change his very form and features. He may readjust the structure of his nervous system and transform the chemistry of his blood. By such changes wrought in himself, he may ripen his corruptible natural body into an incorruptible spiritual body, the perfected fruit of the Tree of Life.

The Ritual of the Pentagram sums up this tremendous aspiration. It states mathematically and Qabalistically the goal and the means. It sets a pattern for self-unfoldment which powerfully influences the operations of the body-building and function-controlling powers of the subconsciousness. It puts us symbolically in right relation to the One Life, and when we are in this right relation, no hostile influence can possibly injure us.

Automatically, this ritual produces the conditions, both physical and astral which make easier for us the realization of our true place in the universal scheme. You are admonished to make yourself familiar with all the details of its meaning.

The Sacred Ritual of the Pentagram

There are depths of significance below the surface of the written word of this instruction. Enough has been said to enable you to know what the ritual means, and what it is intended to accomplish. Understanding of its deeper values is the fruit of careful, intelligent and faithful practice of the Ritual itself.

* * *

NOTE FROM AIMA: The material in this chapter has been gathered after much research in many volumes and from various other sources. Among the volumes consulted credit should go to: *Transcendental Magic* by Eliphas Levi. The four volumes by Israel Regardie entitled *The Golden Dawn,* and his book *The Middle Pillar, Magick in Theory and Practice* by Aleister Crowley, and others too numerous to list here.

[NOTE FROM THE EDITOR: The descriptions of the four archangels were added from *The Magician: His Training and Work* by W.E. Butler, Wilshire Book Company, 1973. Butler derived these from standard Golden Dawn attributions. Israel Regardie's *Golden Dawn* is now available in an updated and expanded edition from New Falcon Publications as *The Complete Golden Dawn System of Magic.*

We have diligently sought after information on the Nagle sisters but have thus far been unable to locate their heirs. It was however deemed so important to preserve this teaching that is being offered here with some additional editing. Any information on the Nagle sisters would be greatly appreciated by the editor and publisher.]

A Pentagram Exercise
Lon Milo DuQuette

Those who regard this ritual as a mere device to invoke or banish spirits are unworthy to possess it. Properly understood, it is the Medicine of Metals and the Stone of the Wise.

—Aleister Crowley[1]

The rituals of the Pentagram (both the Lesser and the Greater rituals) are among the first ceremonies recommended for the beginning magician. Mastery of the Pentagram is tantamount to mastery of the microcosmic universe of one's own body and physical environment. What more fitting and necessary place for us to begin the Great Work—a journey designed to expand the magician's consciousness from the Pentagram's elemental world step-by-step through the planetary heavens embodied by Hexagram, and beyond to the most transcendent and ineffable realms of being.

---

1 Aleister Crowley. *Collected Works of Aleister Crowley.* "The Palace of the World." Chicago, IL: Yoga Publication Society. (1974).

A Pentagram Exercise

Volumes have been written about the power of the Pentagram and the importance of the rituals based upon the secrets of its construction. I would like to share with you just one simple meditative exercise that I've developed over the years—one small facet of the great jewel of the Pentagram.

Before I describe the exercise I remind the reader there are *twelve* Pentagrams in all. These are determined by the number of ways the complete figure may be "drawn" by starting at any given point and tracing in either a clockwise or counterclockwise direction. The alert reader will be quick to correctly observe that there are only *ten* ways to draw the five-pointed Pentagram in this manner. But, as you will soon see the Pentagram that banishes Water is also used to invoke Air; and the Pentagram that banishes Air is also used to invoke Water.[2] Keeping this phenomenon in mind find there are:

- **Eight Elemental Pentagrams**—one to invoke and one to banish each of the four Elements (Fire, Water, Air, and Earth). The general rule of thumb when drawing an Elemental Pentagram is to invoke *toward* and banish *away* from the elemental point in question.

[Note: The eight Elemental Pentagrams are drawn in such a way as to avoid violating on the first stroke the "groin" angle below and opposite the "head/Spirit" point of the Pentagram. This fact will become very

---

2 Although I've read many occult and recondite commentaries on this "mystery" of Air and Water, Regardie once told me it was simply a matter of the *"economy of geometry."*

important when we consider the nature of the Spirit Pentagrams and our exercise.]

- **Four Spirit Pentagrams**—one to invoke and one to banish the Pentagram of Spirit Active—one to invoke and one to banish the Pentagram of Spirit Passive.

  [Note: Spirit has dual role to play in the elemental universe. Like magnetism itself, Spirit 1) *pulls* the four Elements together in their infinite ratios and combinations to form all things in the natural universe; 2) *pushes* the four Elements apart so that they do not smash so close together that they loose their individual elemental natures. This double-duty is why there are Invoking and Banishing Pentagrams for Spirit *Active*, and Invoking and Banishing Pentagrams for Spirit *Passive*.

In the Lesser Pentagram Rituals the magician works with only the eight Elemental Pentagrams. However, in the Greater (or Supreme) rituals of the Pentagram, the Spirit Pentagrams are also used (the Spirit Active Pentagram to accompany the *Active* Elements of Fire and Air; the Spirit Passive Pentagrams to accompany the *Passive* Elements of Water and Earth).

The classic rituals of the Pentagram oblige the magician to physically stand in the center of the temple and draw (with the wand, sword, incense stick, finger, etc.) the appropriate Pentagrams in the air while he or she visualizes them suspended in the air. This is a wonderful ceremony that accom-

A Pentagram Exercise

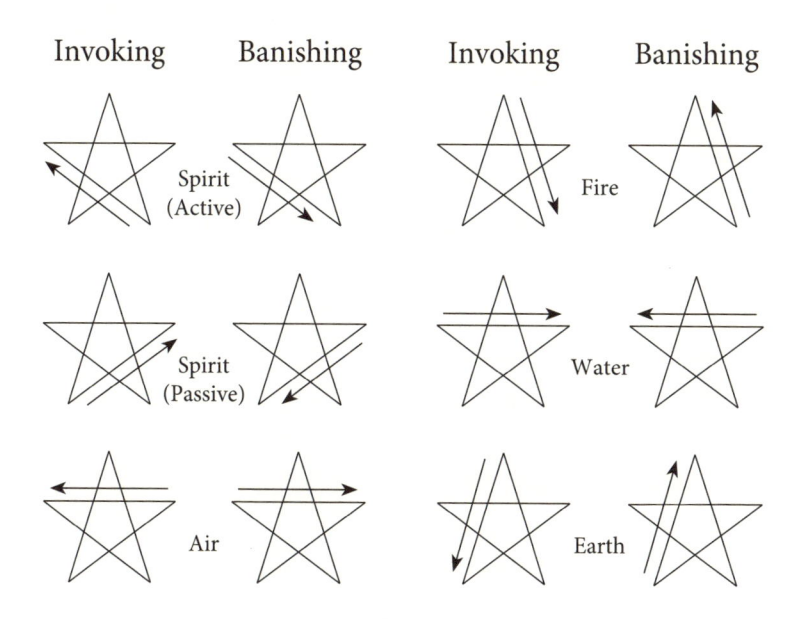

Invoking	Banishing	Invoking	Banishing
Spirit (Active)		Fire	
Spirit (Passive)		Water	
Air		Earth	

The Twelve Pentagrams

plishes many things especially the development of the magician's all-important powers of visualization. In these rituals the magician draws these Pentagrams just as he or she would if upon an imaginary blackboard or upright tablet. In the exercise I am about to show you, however, you will not be dealing with the Pentagrams as if you were drawing them in the air around you, but rather, *you* will actually *become* the Pentagram, and run the various Elemental energies through your own body as if you were invoking or banishing them upon yourself.

This is done (at least at first) by laying down on your back on the floor, exercise mat, or bed—your arms stretched straight out to your sides (crucifixion style), your legs

The Human Figure and the Pentagram

straight and spread so your feet are separated as far apart as is comfortable.

In this position your head represents Spirit; your right hand Air; your left hand Water; your right foot is Earth; your left foot is Fire.

The ultimate object of this exercise is to transform yourself, body, mind, and psychic bodies, into the complete and perfectly balanced microcosmic man or woman—to make you, as it were, a walking Pentagram with all its powers, potentials, and attributes. The exercise is so simple I need only to give one detailed example in order for you to get the idea and understand the process for all twelve Pentagrams. For our example I will use the invoking and banish Pentagrams of Earth.

A Pentagram Exercise

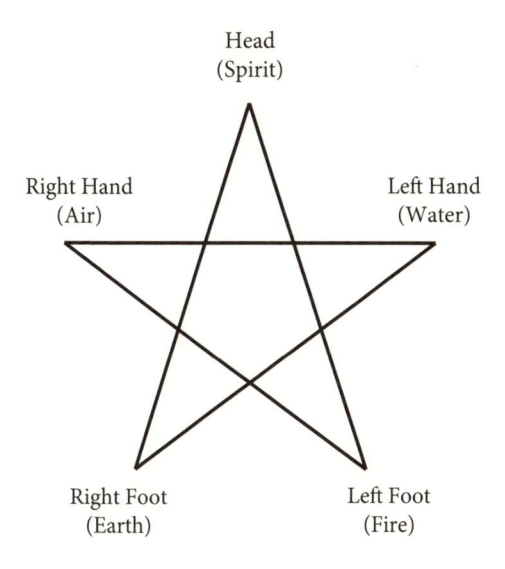

```
            Head
           (Spirit)
              /\
             /  \
Right Hand  /    \  Left Hand
  (Air)    /      \  (Water)
         /‾‾‾‾‾‾‾‾\
         \  /\  /
          \/  \/
          /\  /\
         /  \/  \
Right Foot      Left Foot
 (Earth)         (Fire)
```

The Elements of the Pentagram Projected Upon Your Body

To invoke the energies of Earth upon your body, lie on your back and form the pentagram—your arms stretched straight out to your sides (crucifixion style), your legs straight but spread so your feet are separated as far apart as is comfortable.

Concentrate for a moment on the center of your forehead (this is where you will begin to draw the invoking Earth Pentagram). Imagine the center of your forehead illuminated by a bright green light. When you have this image visualized clearly in your mind's eye, project that light as a green ray shooting directly from the *center of your forehead* down to the toes of your *right foot* bathing it in a burst of green light. Immediately project the ray up through your groin and across your body to the palm of your *left hand* illuminating

EARTH (a Passive Element)
INVOKING

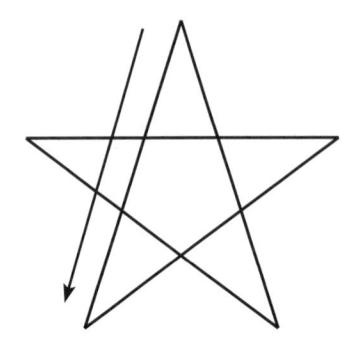

Invoking Pentagram of Earth

it in a burst of green light; now visualize the ray shooting straight across your shoulders to the palm of your *right hand* bathing it in a burst of green light.

Now project the ray of light down and across your body, through your groin, to your *left foot* bathing in burst of green light. Finally, project the light from your left foot up to close the pentagram where it began at center of your *forehead*. Keep the entire pentagram alive with the moving green light as you repeat the process until it courses around the Pentagram smoothly and seemingly independent of your conscious efforts to direct it.

To banish Earth upon your body, lie on your back and form the pentagram. Concentrate for a moment on your *right foot*. Wiggle your toes and imagine them illuminated by a bright green light. When you have this image pictured clearly

A Pentagram Exercise

EARTH (a Passive Element)
BANISHING

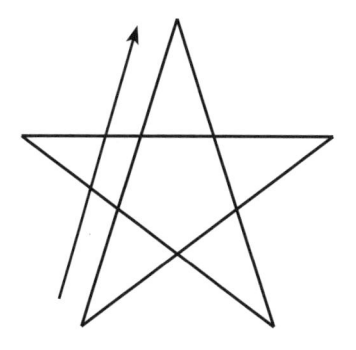

Banishing Pentagram of Earth

in your mind's eye, project that light as a green ray shooting directly from your *right foot* to the *center of your forehead* bathing it in a burst of green light. Immediately project the ray down to the toes of your *left foot* bathing it in a burst of green light; continue extending the ray from your *left foot* up through your groin and across your body to the palm of your *right hand* illuminating it in a burst of green light; now visualize the ray shooting straight across your shoulders to the palm of your *left hand* bathing it in a burst of green light. Finally, project the ray of light down and across your body, through your groin, to close the pentagram where it began at your *right foot*. Keep the entire pentagram alive with the moving green light as you repeat the process until it courses smoothly and seemingly independent of your conscious efforts to direct it.

To invoke and banish the other Pentagrams simply start at the appropriate point of your body's Pentagram and run the elemental current through your body as described above.

The color of the light rays should vary with each Elemental Pentagram. For Fire visualize a *red* ray of light; for Water a *blue* ray; for Air a *yellow* ray; for Earth a *green* ray; and for Spirit a *brilliant white* ray.

SUGGESTED ROUTINE—Part I

Practice whenever is convenient for you. It is best to practice when you are not overly tired or too soon after a meal. I strongly suggest you first work with the Elemental Pentagrams one at a time until your visualization is strong and you can actually feel the elemental current coursing through and around your body. Each Pentagram should have its own unique effect upon your body, thoughts, and dreams. Make detailed notes of these effects. Once you are familiar with how each particular Pentagram makes you feel, try to induce that specific feeling throughout the day. Get comfortable switching these unique feelings on and off at will. Here is a suggested routine.

Week One—Earth:
Each morning for a week practice the green invoking Pentagram of Earth; each evening practice the green banishing Pentagram of Earth.

Week Two—Air:
Each morning and evening for a week do the same with the yellow Pentagrams of Air.

A Pentagram Exercise

Week Three—Water:
Each morning and evening for a week do the same with the blue Pentagrams of Water.

Week One—Fire:
Each morning and evening for a week do the same with the red Pentagrams of Fire.

SUGGESTED ROUTINE—Part II
After you have mastered the exercises of Part I and you are cognizant of the unique feelings and effects each Elemental Pentagram produces. Start including the addition of the appropriate Spirit Pentagram. You should draw the white *Spirit Active* Pentagrams prior to the Pentagrams of Fire and Air (the active Elements); and you should draw the white *Spirit Passive* Pentagrams prior to the Pentagrams of Water and Earth (the passive Elements).

> [Note: In order to draw the Invoking Spirit Pentagram you will be required do something that you have not done before when working with the 8 Elemental Pentagrams. As you draw the ray of white light up either from your *left foot* (for the Invoking Pentagram of Spirit Active), or your *right foot* (for the Invoking Pentagram of Spirit Passive) the first place on your body the light will penetrate is your groin area.]

The first time I did this I noticed something very dramatic as the ray of light passed through this area of my body. My *base chakra* (the Muladhara, lowest of the chakras, located in the region between the genitals and the anus) was severely stimulated and seemed to whirl with an almost tangible vibration. At the exact same instant my *crown chakra* (the Sahasrara, highest of the chakras located at the top of the head) seemed to burst with an electrical tingling that linked itself to my base chakra and slowly ascended up my spine until my whole body was "alight." It was quite wonderful, and a little scary. I then realized the profound relationship between the extremes of the Pentagram (the *point* and *groin* of the Pentagram) and the highest and the lowest chakras of the human psychic body. It is an understatement to say this gave me a new respect for this seemingly simple meditative exercise.

When dealing with the eight Elemental Pentagrams the tip of the Pentagram is at the center of one's forehead, the Ajna (second from the top) chakra. But when invoking Spirit Active or Spirit Passive one can transcend the Ajna and actually activate the highest of all the psychic centers.

The routine for Part II is exactly the same as for Part I except you draw two Pentagrams per Element: A Spirit Active Pentagram proceeding Fire and Air Pentagrams; and a Spirit Passive Pentagram proceeding Water and Earth Pentagrams.

CUSTOS RERUM SAPIENTIA